REA

**DO NOT REMOVE
CARDS FROM POCKET**

Science of Triathlon Training and Competition

Glenn P. Town, PhD

Wheaton College

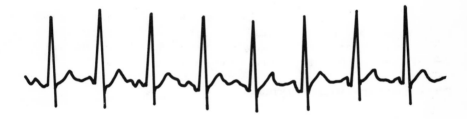

Human Kinetics Publishers, Inc.
Champaign, Illinois

Library of Congress Cataloging in Publication Data

Town, Glenn P., 1949-
    The science of triathlon training and competition.

    Bibliography: p.
    Includes index.
    1. Triathlon—Training. 2. Triathlon—Psychological
aspects. 3. Triathlon—Physiological aspects. I. Title.
GV1060.7.T69 1985   796.4'07   84-25259
ISBN 0-931250-82-X

Production Director: Karen Morse
Developmental Editor: Susan Wilmoth, PhD
Typesetter: Aurora Garcia
Text Layout: Janet K. Davenport
Cover Design and Layout: Jeff Barnes

ISBN: 0-931250-82-X

Printed in the United States of America

10 9 8 7 6 5 4 3 2 1

Human Kinetics Publishers, Inc.
Box 5076, Champaign, IL 61820

Dedication

Who ever said the triathlon is an individual sport? Although I was the only one to wear No. 999 in the Ironman, I am quick to realize there would have been no Ironman for me without the help and support of so many. I, therefore, wish to dedicate this book to all those who gave of their time, talent, and money to fuel a dream into reality.

Highest praise and appreciation is extended to my wife, Nancy, who supported, endured, and shared in all phases of my Ironman experience. Deepest gratitude is also extended to my coach, training partner, and friend, Don Holwerda for his multidimensional commitment to me; to my fund raising chairman Dr. David Gieser, who never once doubted the project's purpose; to Art Heerwagen, who filmed my experience and transformed it into a multimedia presentation which has added an outreach dimension to the entire effort; to Wheaton College, for its faithful support and for giving me the time away to train and compete; and to the legion of friends who believed in the project and lifted me up in prayer from start to finish. Finally, to the Lord Jesus who, through it all, was my source and my strength. (Isaiah 40:29-31)

Acknowledgments

This writing has been my biggest laboratory experience ever. It represents theory that has been tested and failed, as well as theory that has been reinforced by success. As with all theories, only when it stands up to the test of time does it become law. I, therefore, wish to acknowledge those who gave my ideas a chance, for without their feedback this product would have never been finalized.

The following people were very helpful with their suggestions, support, and editing efforts: Don Holwerda, Bill Favata, Dr. Stephen Cushman, Dr. Carl Foster, Art Heerwagen, and Bill McGinty. Jeff Barnes was the genius behind the cover design which creatively suggests the overall theme of the book. Appreciation is also extended to the Human Kinetics staff and especially my editor Susan Wilmoth for her commitment to the project. Thanks also goes to Walt Danylak for taking the photographs for Chapter 6, and Wendy Gieser for the art work throughout the text.

Contents

Introduction

Science of Triathlon Training and Competition

The triathlon has been called one of the most grueling contests ever devised by man to test not only the physical limits of his total body, but the outer limits of his mental endurance as well. Consisting of swimming, bicycling, and running, the triathlon event also tests the versatility of the athlete. Because the event requires such versatility, the "elite" athlete tends to become neutralized with the "all-around" performer finding success. This quality offers most people the opportunity of doing well. Regarded by many as the ultimate physical test, the focus has become one of finishing; to that end, everyone can be a winner!

For centuries man has been challenged to pursue the outer limits of his physical and mental endurance. Suggest a means of transportation, both physical and mechanical, and somewhere an attempt has been made to discover its elusive boundaries. In recent times people have become more aware of their bodies. Associated with this awareness has been this individual challenge of the body's limits. For example, in the 1970s, the marathon road race became a very popular challenge for runners of all abilities. Foremost, the victory was in finishing, and during the past decade, thousands of runners attempted and conquered this endurance test. However, the marathon "mystique" no longer exists.

Quite possibly it is this marathon running craze that has opened up such a favorable response to the triathlon challenge. If the early years of 1980 offer us any prediction about the future of triathlons, we can safely assume the event is here to stay.

Conceived out of a barroom discussion of who was the fittest—the swimmer, the cyclist, or the runner—the answer was ultimately decided by combining all three. Existing Hawaiian endurance courses in all three events became the criterion, and in 1978, 15 men competed in the first of what is now known as the Ironman World Championships. Since that date, interest has gained momentum to the point where 1,250 competitors were accepted in the 1984 event with most of them meeting stringent qualifying standards.

In terms of nationwide popularity, in 1982 approximately 60,000 people competed in more than 200 multisport events across the country. Efforts to become an organized, sanctioned event have culminated in the formation of the United States Triathlon Series (USTS) which sponsored five professional events in 1982, each at the sanctioned distances of a 2 kilometer swim, a 35 kilometer bicycling event, and a 15 kilometer run. The 1983 series expanded to include USTS events in eight major cities across the United States with regional winners competing in a USTS National Championship at Bass Lake, California. In the 1983 USTS series, 6,316 people participated. The 1984 USTS series expanded to include two more major cities, but reduced the distances to a 1.5 kilometer swim, a 40 kilometer bike, and a 10 kilometer run. Current interest in triathlons as an international competitive sport is intense, even to the point of considering the triathlon as a future olympic event.

With all the growing interest in a sport with such a promising future, one would assume that volumes of research and training manuals would abound in efforts to serve such a population. Ironically, published literature is void of scientific investigation related specifically to the triathlon. Of the more than 400 research papers presented at the National American College of Sports Medicine Conventions in 1982 and in 1984, not one person addressed the intricacies concerning the triathlon. The same conference in 1983 presented two papers on the triathlon. Maybe it is assumed that the volumes of written material related to swimming, cycling, and running, each as separate entities, are sufficient information to allow for a safe and effective combining effort. Indeed, the research available in each of these events is valuable to the triple-sport competitor. However, this information is far from complete when one reviews the unique characteristics of the sport. Unanswered questions include How can one train for three sports simultaneously without injury or mental and physical burnout? What are the physical and metabolic demands experienced when one transfers from one sport modality to another without rest; and How can stored energy be carefully distributed over extremely long periods of time?

Successful completion of the triathlon event is only as effective as the preparation time invested. How one prepares for competition should be approached systematically and scientifically with attention given to both the obvious and discreet concerns related to the event. These and many other unique characteristics of the triathlon event are carefully investigated in the following pages.

Chapter 1

Physiological Concerns of Performance

Any athlete involved in an endurance sport, at any level, should have a basic understanding of how the body responds, adapts, recovers, and regulates when exposed to chronic (long-term, regular) exercise. Without this basic understanding, training will inevitably lack direction, focus, and rationale. So often athletes pursue a new concept in training without the ability to discern how, where, or even if this new concept should be applied to their training program. The purpose of this chapter is to introduce you to the necessary physiology of sport performance which will enable you to follow the logic of this book, and also to allow you to better evaluate personal application to present and future concepts related to sport performance.

Energy Production

Energy Systems

All functions of the human body, regardless of their complexity, require energy to operate. Even to digest the energy-providing foods we eat, energy must be made available. For the athlete concerned with sport performance, the energy needed to create and sustain muscle contraction is of great concern. The chemical reaction which liberates the energy needed before muscle will contract is the breakdown of Adenosine Triphosphate (ATP) to Adenosine Diphosphate (ADP). Figure 1.1 illustrates this reaction.

As long as ATP is available at the site of muscle contraction, movement can occur. However, the problem with this simple reaction is that ATP is only available in very limited amounts. What must occur, therefore, is the resynthesis of ADP and the broken-off phosphate back into ATP. Three different energy systems which are capable of resynthesizing ADP + P into ATP have been identified in the body. The three systems are the fast-acting phosphocreatine system (ATP-PC); the intermediate lactic acid (LA) or anaerobic glycolysis system; and the slowest system to produce energy—the aerobic system. Whenever muscles contract, all three systems go into operation at the same time, but ATP output occurs at varying rates depending on the complexity and number of reactions needed in each system.

Let's examine the interrelationships of these three systems as they supply the energy for a bicycle ride from moderate to intense speeds through some rolling hills. Before mounting your bike, assume the body is in a state of rest and at full recovery. In this condition, the body's need for oxygen and energy are adequately being met, or in other words, the supply equals the demand. During the first few minutes of the ride, you pedal along effortlessly, but it's not long before your breathing becomes heavier and your legs begin to experience pain. The two energy systems (ATP-PC and LA), which do not require oxygen to produce energy, are filling the needs of muscle contraction during this early phase of exercise.

The first energy system to be activated is the phosphocreatine (PC) system. This system requires only one chemical reaction before ATP is regenerated and once again available as an energy source for muscle contraction. The problem, however, is that the PC system can only resynthesize a very small amount of ADP to ATP. Consequently, it can only contribute to the energy needs of muscle contraction for a few seconds.

While the PC system is operating, a second energy system is also activated. This system, called the lactic acid cycle, is an 11-step chemical reaction that generates small amounts of ATP but requires blood glucose (a simple sugar) to do so. The lactic acid cycle picks up where the PC system leaves off and is capable of supplying the energy needed for muscle contraction for approximately 1 minute of high-intensity exercise.

The lactic acid system is also known as *anaerobic glycolysis,* a term which signifies the ability to break down glucose (glycolysis) without the presence of

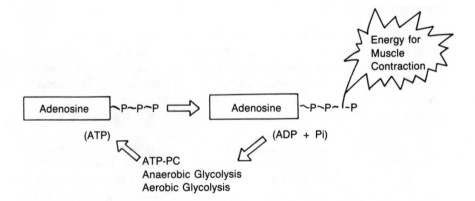

Figure 1.1 Breakdown and rebuilding of the ATP molecule.

oxygen (anaerobic). Anaerobic glycolysis is extremely important to us during exercise, primarily because this system provides energy upon quick demand. Without this system, cycling up steep hills or performing sprinting strategies would not be possible.

So far, we've performed our cycling tour without the need of our most valuable nutrient—oxygen. This is the real concern not only to our bicyclist, but to all athletes who require their muscles to contract for long periods of time. When oxygen is available during exercise, glucose continues to be broken down through a more complex aerobic cycle which requires hundreds of additional steps. Even though the aerobic system engages as soon as you apply force on the pedals, the multitude of reactions that must be completed before energy is predominantly supplied aerobically takes at least 1 minute. This apparent disadvantage is in no way a limitation in endurance performance since the lactic acid system is compensating for the delay. Once into the aerobic system, our bicycle ride continues with great efficiency, usually in a seemingly effortless fashion.

Benefits of the Aerobic System

The benefits of exercising in the aerobic system are truly remarkable and are of great importance to the triple sport athlete. Efficiency is the first benefit of working in the aerobic system. The amount of energy produced from a molecule of glucose by the anaerobic glycolysis system is only 5% of what could be produced by the same molecule if processed aerobically. In a sport where so much of one's success or failure hinges on the energy available for muscle contraction, this comparison becomes of key importance.

The second important benefit to exercising aerobically is that three different fuels—fats, carbohydrates, and certain portions of the protein chain (called amino acids)—can be used to produce muscle contraction. In contrast, the anaerobic glycolysis system can use only glucose from the carbohydrates to produce energy. Since the brain can receive its energy needs only from carbohydrates, the need to conserve on this "brain food" becomes apparent.

The third benefit of exercising aerobically deals with the end products of metabolism. Here, the end products of aerobically processed glucose are energy (and lots of it), water (which can be used in other areas of metabolism), and carbon dioxide (which is released into the atmosphere with each exhalation). The end product of anaerobic glycolysis is a small amount of energy, carbon dioxide, and lactic acid, a chemical which greatly contributes to fatigue and limits the body's ability to contract muscle efficiently. Once the aerobic system is engaged, one experiences a more comfortable breathing rate along with the ability to continue exercising for longer periods of time.

Let us continue our discussion of the lactic acid problem by introducing the term *anaerobic threshold.* The anaerobic threshold is the point where the exercise intensity increases to a level where more oxygen is required than the body can provide. In other words, the oxygen supply is simply not able to meet the oxygen demand. At this point, the anaerobic glycolysis system (lactic acid system) is engaged, allowing muscle contraction to continue. As illustrated in Figure 1.2, levels of lactic acid remain low until such a point when the oxygen available is not enough to effectively process energy aerobically. At the anaerobic threshold, levels of lactic acid in the blood and muscle begin to rise exponentially.

Although we can continue to exercise, the increased presence of lactic acid creates havoc with the body's ability to perform efficient muscle contraction. Because lactic acid (as its name implies) is an acid, the usual neutral condition that the body maintains becomes acidic when lactic acid is present in large quantities. Furthermore, when the environment for producing energy becomes acidic, the rate at which energy can be provided is greatly reduced. When exceeding your anaerobic threshold, you, as an athlete, feel muscle pain, strained breathing, and fatigue.

Fatigue is a problem of special concern to the triathlete. Keeping lactic acid at low levels will contribute greatly toward preventing the premature onset of fatigue. Endurance athletes have coined fatigue carried to the limit as "the wall." Besides lactic acid, several other factors can bring about the dreaded "wall" endurance athletes so carefully try to avoid. These factors include (a) depletion of muscle glycogen stores (carbohydrate depletion), (b) dehydration, (c) a loss of electrolytes (potassium and salts), (d) hyperthermia (increased body temperature), and (e) plain old boredom. The fate of how these factors influence fatigue rests in the hands of the athlete and, therefore, will receive further comment in the chapters dealing with nutrition and training techniques.

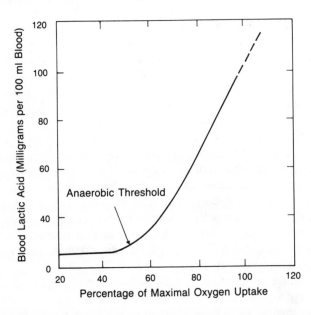

Figure 1.2 Anaerobic threshold curve. From *Physiology of Fitness* (p. 12) by B.J. Sharkey, 1979, Champaign, IL: Human Kinetics Publishers. Reprinted by permission.

Chronic Exercise Considerations

Chronic exercise promotes physiological changes in the body as a result of training. When the body is exposed to physical demands on a regular basis (at least three times weekly), certain adaptations take place that make the physical demands more tolerable to the body's systems; familiar examples include reduced muscle soreness, increased muscle tone, and a loss in fat mass. The ways in which the body deals with the problems of efficiency and fatigue as a result of chronic exercise are discussed next.

Efficiency

An oversized engine in an automobile will provide a healthy surge of power when you occasionally need it but under normal use will give you poor gas mileage. With today's problems of high-priced gasoline, manufacturers are constantly improving on engine design to generate more miles to the gallon. If increased mileage and a larger gas tank were paired together, the ability to travel long distances would be realized.

Both of these concerns—efficient energy utilization and increased storage of fuels—are handled in a remarkable way when the human body is exposed to regular exercise of proper intensity, frequency, and duration. The physiological changes which produce these desirable improvements occur in almost every system of the body but particularly in the skeletal muscles and the cardiorespiratory system.

When we speak of the efficiency of aerobic performance, two concerns arise: (a) getting large quantities of oxygen and nutrients to the contracting muscle quickly, and (b) the ability of the muscle to process these materials into usable energy.

Transporting oxygen and nutrients to the muscle site is a cooperative effort between the central circulatory system (heart) and the peripheral circulatory system, which consists of the capillary network surrounding every living cell in the body. With training, the heart pumps blood in greater quantities with each contraction. This improvement is accomplished through an increase in the size of one of the heart's chambers (left ventricle), but without the dangerous thickening of the chamber walls. Along with this change is the heart's ability to eject blood from the heart more completely. You, the exerciser, notice these changes in the form of a decreased resting heart rate.

At the receiving end of this supply system is the skeletal muscle. Here, a remarkable change occurs when muscles are exercised aerobically. The microscopic blood vessels called capillaries, which deliver blood to each cell, are multiplied. This increases the availability of the chemicals and fuels needed to maintain muscle contraction. Also, this increased vascularization has tremendous implications in dealing with the dreaded lactic acid problem and will be discussed later.

In an effort to deal with the now abundant supply of oxygen and nutrients, cells increase their ability to convert the nutrients into usable energy. This is accomplished by increasing the number and size of miniature energy factories called mitochondria within each cell, plus increasing the amount of chemicals (enzymes) necessary to do the job. Realize, however, that these physical improvements occur only when greater-than-normal demands are placed on the aerobic energy system.

Proper training will also increase the body's ability to store more energy nutrients. How the body uses both fats and carbohydrates to produce energy will be discussed later, but realize for now that these fuels are necessary for continued muscle contraction. Long-term muscle contraction requires the ability to store these fuels in great quantities and also to make these fuels readily available. Past studies indicate that trained endurance athletes have intramuscular fat stores 1.5 times greater than untrained males and females (Hoppeler, Luthi, Claasen, Weibel, & Howald, 1973). These fat stores serve one additional benefit: When fats are readily available, the body tends to use them instead of relying heavily on valuable and limited amounts of carbohydrates. This concept of conserving carbohydrates is called the glycogen-sparing effect.

With systematic training, the body can store even more carbohydrates: The exercised muscles can store as much as 2.5 times more than an untrained muscle (Gollnick et al. 1973). It is easy to see how the improvements in energy production and greater fuel stores work together in effectively improving all aspects of aerobic capacity.

It is important to note that these metabolic improvements occur only in the muscles being exercised. Carbohydrates stored in the upper body, for instance, cannot be called upon to serve the needs of exercising leg muscles. This concept will be treated later in the training methods chapter.

Lactic Acid

Lactic acid is not the villain of all aerobic exercises, but rather plays an important role in physical exertion. Movement from rest to exercise, as well as any acceleration during exercise, would be severely hindered without this quick energy-producing system. Apart from these important roles, the accumulation of lactic acid should be carefully avoided since it makes such inefficient use of valuable carbohydrate stores, and its acidic nature limits performance.

The human body responds remarkably to repeated exposures to this sometimes dreaded by-product of energy production. With training, several efficient changes occur in the body which (a) decrease lactic acid production, and (b) increase the removal rate of lactic acid from the bloodstream where it can be reconverted into usable fuel at the liver.

The major way in which the body decreases lactic acid production is by increasing the anaerobic threshold. Note in Figure 1.3, the anaerobic threshold (the work intensity at which lactic acid begins to accumulate) is around 60% of the maximum aerobic capacity in untrained subjects, but is about 75% in trained distance runners.

Note also that the anaerobic threshold of Derek Clayton, once the world's fastest marathoner, is very close to 85% of his maximum aerobic capacity. This suggests that with training, the body will allow you to work at greater capacities without accumulating toxic levels of lactic acid.

A second way in which lactic acid levels are kept to a minimum occurs at the onset of exercise. As you remember, going from rest to exercise is primarily performed in the anaerobic state. The trained body shortens the transition from anaerobic to aerobic metabolism and this results in smaller quantities of lactic acid.

The trained body is also capable of removing lactic acid as it is produced. In total aerobic exercise, lactic acid production and removal occur at the same rate. This is evidenced by the near resting levels of lactic acid in marathoners at the *end* of their race (Costill, Thomason, & Roberts, 1973). Even when these levels increase, the conditioned body is still capable of processing lactic acid back into a usable fuel. Finally, the aerobically trained individual is capable of tolerating higher levels of this toxic end-product. This is especially valuable as the triathlete makes the transition from one event to another.

In summary, an aerobically conditioned body produces smaller amounts of LA during exercise, is capable of exercising at higher levels without as much LA production, can tolerate LA in greater amounts, and can better remove that LA which is produced. These are important considerations for the triathlete who must conserve energy whenever possible.

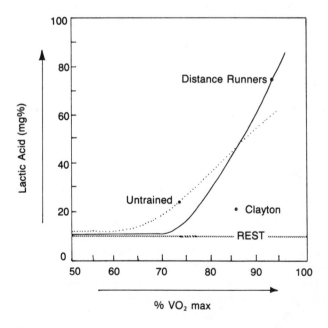

Figure 1.3 Anaerobic thresholds of trained and untrained subjects compared. From *The Physiological Basis of Physical Education and Athletics*, 3rd edition (p. 310) by E.L. Fox and D.K. Mathews, 1981, Philadelphia: Saunders College Publishing. Reprinted by permission.

Heat Acclimatization

Any machine capable of producing movement will generate an energy by-product in the form of heat. In fact, heat production is one of the ways in which efficiency is evaluated: the more efficient, the less heat produced. Even the most efficient machinery such as the diesel engine is only about 50% efficient. This means that of all the energy available to produce work, half will be used to produce the desired outcome with the remaining half given off in the form of heat. An athlete, in excellent form and in the greatest condition, is still only capable of producing about a 30% efficiency rate. So even in the best of circumstances, a tremendous amount of heat is generated through muscle contraction. Studies have shown that in intense exercise using large muscle groups, the body can produce as much as 70 times the heat it does at rest. If this excess heat is not dissipated, the body temperature will generally rise, even to the point where performance will be compromised or even terminated.

Some heat is released from the body through respiration and urination; but, the most important way to release heat is through the skin. The body performs this internal cooling task much like the cooling system in your car: a water pump pushes water through a network of channels within your engine, drawing heat out of the deepest portions of the engine and into the circulating water or coolant (see Figure 1.4). The heated liquid then leaves the engine and is channeled through the radiator where the liquid is cooled by the air passing around the radiator. Once cooled, the fluid is then ready for another tour through the engine.

The human body has the same basic cooling system, but in a much more complex way. The pump, of course, is the heart, and the coolant is the plasma portion of the blood. Since blood circulates in close proximity to all living cells, it removes excess heat from the active tissues, namely skeletal muscle.

After leaving the active tissue, the blood then moves through a specialized capillary network in the skin's surface called the venous plexus. These capillaries are in close contact with the atmosphere where the heat is finally dissipated.

Depending on the temperature and humidity difference between the skin and the atmosphere, the amount of heat the skin emits into the atmosphere varies greatly. When the body temperature is greater than the surrounding atmosphere, a favorable temperature gradient is established, whereby the heat is simply given off into the atmosphere. Heat given off in this manner is called radiation. A second way in which the body releases its excess heat is by convection. This process involves air or water passing over the body which then draws the heat away from the body if a desirable temperature gradient is established.

During exercise, the major portion of heat loss is through evaporation of sweat from the body's surface. Blood still approaches the skin's surface as previously described; in addition, the sweat mechanism triggers water to emerge on the skin's surface where it must be changed into water vapor. This transfer of energy from liquid to gas cools the skin. However, if sweat is produced at a rate faster than it can be evaporated, then this process of cooling breaks down. Evaporation must involve changing sweat from a liquid to a gaseous form. In high humidity and/or high temperature environments, sweat is frequently produced at rates greater than what is being evaporated, often to the extent where as much as a gallon of sweat is lost per hour!

Most of us realize that we should slow down our workouts when confronted with a hot and humid environment, but we might not understand the rationale behind such a recommendation. Because blood is shunted to the skin's surface for cooling, 15 to 25% less blood is available for the exercising muscles. Therefore, continuing to exercise with this compromised blood supply will create high levels of fatigue.

The second concern is with the components of sweat itself, namely water and salt. Next to the air we breathe, water is the most important nutrient of our body. In terms of the cooling process, water serves as a tremendous heat sink. Water absorbs great amounts of heat without significantly raising its temperature. Water also serves as the main component of sweat. In this capacity, water is sacrificed from several sites in the body, but the site that is of greatest concern is the circulating blood. Fifty-five percent of our total blood volume is a watery substance called plasma. The water content of this substance is readily given up for sweat production which creates a reduction in total blood volume and thickens the blood that remains. These changes will have an adverse effect on performance unless body fluids are replenished quickly and adequately. Should dehydration be neglected, serious heat-related illnesses can result.

To avoid dehydration, water must be adequately replaced as soon as the exercise bout begins. Many athletes wait until they become thirsty, which is much too late. Since the thirst mechanism is a delayed response, exercisers can be as much as 50% dehydrated before they feel the need to drink. Between 100 and 200 ml (3 to 6.5 oz) of water should be taken at 10 to 15 minute intervals throughout the activity.

Dehydration prevention should be part of your training program in order to learn how much water you can consume without getting stomach cramps or feeling bloated. Carry a water bottle while running, and choose a route where you can refill once or twice every hour.

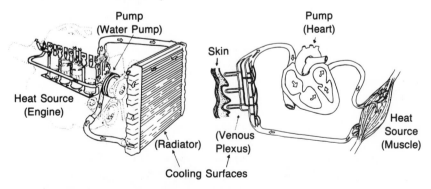

Figure 1.4 Cooling systems of an automobile engine compared to the human body's cooling system.

Salt imbalances (namely, sodium, potassium, and chloride) can also result when excess sweating occurs. Normal diets will adequately supply the body with these salts, but abnormally heavy sweating over long periods of exercise may require supplementation. A safe policy for exercisers who regularly confront the heat would be to liberally salt their foods at mealtimes. Salt tablet consumption is strongly discouraged because this megadose situation can create severe dehydration.

Techniques for Heat Acclimatization

The major acclimatization occurs during the first week of heat exposure and is essentially complete by the end of 10 days. Only 2 to 4 hours of daily heat exposure are required. Start the acclimatization process by exposing yourself to light workouts lasting about 15 to 20 minutes. After a few of these sessions, increases in intensity and duration can follow. Remember, full heat acclimatization cannot be achieved without actual exposure to heat.

What happens physiologically is quite interesting. For one thing, training increases the sensitivity of the sweating response so that sweating begins at a lower body temperature. An increase in sweat output also occurs which will maximize the evaporative cooling process. This greater sweat output contains less salt, so the electrolytes are preserved. All these changes assume that water is being consumed at the same rate it is being given off as sweat—all the more reason for replacing fluids frequently.

The body experiences many other changes when exposed to chronic exercise: For example, bones become harder, tendons become stronger, and muscles become more resistant to tears. All these changes must be viewed as occurring simultaneously. At the same time the body becomes an efficient cooling mechanism, it is also becoming more efficient at supplying the energy nutrients. The body's response to chronic training creates many improvements, provided an adequate stimulus is created to challenge its current physiology to pursue higher levels of efficiency.

Chapter 2

The Fuels for Performance

Those of us who watched Julie Moss's dramatic finish in the February 1982 Ironman were deeply moved by her determination and will power to cross the finish line. This display of sheer guts was an inspiration to many of us to pursue the triathlon challenge. ABC's *Wide World of Sports* noted that their coverage of Julie's struggle to finish was viewed by more people than any other event they filmed that year! I wish to expound on Julie's experience and show how it effectively illustrates the close relationship between the supply and demand that is inherent in this ultraendurance sport.

As I review Julie's effort, several possibilities could explain why she came up short, when only a mile earlier, all indications pointed toward Julie Moss winning the Ironman World Triathlon Championship. What happened? Perhaps the mental anguish became intolerable. Athletes use the term *psyched out* to describe the mental shortcomings that limit performance. Another possibility is that Julie wasn't sufficiently trained to participate in such an enormous event. As coaches often say, she just didn't pay the price in training. Julie could have also experienced dehydration and symptoms of heat stroke, or perhaps, Julie could have simply depleted her energy stores. Athletes call this experience "hitting the wall" or "going bonkers."

Seeing Julie's sheer determination to finish, her agonizing expressions, and her unwillingness to quit was evidence enough to eliminate the possibility that Julie was simply psyched out. Realize also that Julie was enroute to a record performance—more evidence that this woman was well trained for the task she set out to conquer. The possibility of dehydration is certainly a viable one, for the four liters of glucose solution she received intravenously after the race suggest that she was indeed in a fluid deficit. However, to diagnose her limitation as being only a problem of fluid intake would be misrepresenting the total picture. I suggest that Julie Moss exhausted her energy supply before the race demands were met. Energy depletion along with dehydration are common problems that endurance athletes confront regularly while training and competing.

Probably every endurance competitor with the least bit of desire to pursue the outer limits of his or her physical capacities has encountered the "bear, monkey, or wall." I remember moving through the first 20 miles of a hilly East Coast marathon where I hit my exact target pace of 2 hours. By mile 24 I was feeling quite strong and was still right on pace as my split was 2:24. My long eluded goal of completing a marathon at a 6 min/mile pace was close at hand. But shortly after mile 24, I literally came unglued! My legs felt like rubber, my breathing was short and irregular, and my mind was commanding me to retreat. I was given no choice but to merely shuffle through the agonizing 2 miles that remained. I can recall other encounters with this helpless experience, but this one clearly separated the mental from the physical. Fortunately, I had to carry the monkey for only 2 miles; others can tell horror stories of enduring this experience for many more.

This chapter investigates the fuels our bodies use in performance, how these fuels are obtained from our diet, how they are best stored, and how these fuels are most efficiently used. These concerns are extremely important to the triathlete since they directly affect one's success in training and competition; they also can have tremendous impact on injuries and injury recovery. Too often individuals spend considerable time and energy striving for the optimum in exercise performance, only to fall short because of inadequate, counterproductive, and sometimes harmful nutritional practices.

The everyday functions of growth, cell replication, repair, thought, and movement that our bodies perform can occur only when proper quantities of all essential nutrients are made available for the body to use. The term essential implies that the body cannot produce the nutrient by itself, and it must therefore be supplied by the foods we eat. Essential nutrients consist of the three food nutrients, protein, fat, and carbohydrates, as well as vitamins, certain minerals, and water. However, the only essential nutrients that carry any energy-producing value are the three food nutrients: carbohydrates, fats, and proteins. Vitamins and minerals are extremely important, but not as a source of fuel.

Energy Nutrients

To fuel the body and to provide energy efficiently over long durations, all three food nutrients are used. Most athletes consider carbohydrates to be the main fuel in endurance performance with some reliance on fats, with proteins never entering the energy production picture. If this were true, high-level physical performance would last about 2 hours and then require approximately 24 hours to complete the refueling process. With this observation in mind, I would like to discuss the dynamics of the three energy nutrients, how they interrelate, and then introduce some recent research we did on the fuel demands of triathletes.

Carbohydrates

Plant life provides us with our total supply of carbohydrates. Plants assimilate hydrogen, carbon, and oxygen with the sun as a catalyst to produce either simple sugars or complex carbohydrates. The difference between these two substances is the number of sugar molecules which are bonded together. Simple sugars (carbohydrates) consist of either one or two sugar molecules. These can be either single molecules of glucose, fructose, galactose, or the linking of two of these in combination. Complex carbohydrates, on the other hand, link together 300 to 1,000 or more glucose molecules into a chemical chain. When this linking occurs in plants, the carbohydrate chain is called a starch, but in animals it is called glycogen.

Glucose performs a unique and extremely crucial role in the body. Think of glucose as a "general purpose" energy source in the body. It is the only substance that can be used in anaerobic glycolysis, and more importantly, it is the only substance that can serve the energy needs of the brain and nervous system. For these important reasons, glucose is often called blood sugar. Part of the carbohydrate depletion or "bonkers" sensations, which demonstrates the dependence of the brain on glucose, include weakness, hunger, nausea, and dizziness. (Keeping this in mind, I propose we adopt banana sandwiches instead of olives as the new brain food.)

The major problem with carbohydrates as the primary energy source in the body is its limited storage ability. Untrained persons carry only enough carbohydrate reserves to get them through about one day of sedentary activity. Therefore, it is quite easy to see how beginning exercisers can be so fatigued when entering into a new level of activity. With training, however, the ability to store carbohydrates is greatly enhanced, even as much as 2.5 times that of a sedentary individual!

The sites for carbohydrate storage are in the liver, skeletal muscles and blood. The liver serves as a general warehouse for the total body; skeletal muscles only provide fuels for the muscle in which the carbohydrates are stored. Finally, small amounts of glucose exist in the blood itself which is usually in-transit to a cell in need or off to be stored as glycogen. When all glycogen stores are full, the glucose that remains is stored as fat. Glucose has about 24 hours to serve a need or find a spot on a glycogen chain before it is sacrificed to the fat stores. Once this conversion is made, it is very difficult to be reconverted into glucose.

The rate of glucose ingestion is of great concern to the endurance athlete. When carbohydrates are consumed in the form of simple sugars, the digestion process occurs quite rapidly, the sugars entering the bloodstream very quickly. This creates a blood glucose "gush" and triggers the liver to release large amounts of insulin in an effort to clear the high glucose levels from the blood. The insulin released usually overreacts, which in the end, leaves the blood glucose at dangerously low levels. Signs of fatigue, dizziness, and lethargy normally follow.

It is generally believed that the consumption of complex carbohydrates such as breads, potatoes, pasta, and rice do not effect a blood glucose gush but instead allow the glucose to 'trickle' into the bloodstream. However, recent research by Jenkins and colleagues (1981), has demonstrated that many of the complex carbohydrates are taken up in the bloodstream as fast if not faster than table sugar. Pastas were about the only complex carbohydrates that did indeed trickle the glucose molecules into the bloodstream. Athletes who chomp down chocolate bars, take megadoses of dextrose pills, or shovel in the breads and potatoes immediately before competition should expect a compromised performance.

Fats

Fats provide the greatest source of potential energy to our body. Even in people who carry proper amounts of body fat, 90,000 to 100,000 Kcal of energy are held in reserve! If all other systems could remain operable, this tremendous caloric supply would allow an individual to run 900 to 1,000 miles or bike 4,000 miles without refueling! Incredible, yes—but totally impossible! Fats also cushion and protect many of the vital organs of our body and, due to the fat buffer that exists subcutaneously, insulate us from the cold.

A function of fat which should be of great concern to the endurance athlete is that of *glucose sparing*. In a trained athlete, the body develops the ability to sustain long periods of muscle contraction by deriving between 50% and 80% of the energy needs from fats. In doing so, glucose is conserved. This is critical when considering the absolute dependence that the brain has on carbohydrates, especially when realizing the limited carbohydrate reserves the body carries. If you can create an environment for effective utilization of fat stores, there is little to fear.

Realize that the anaerobic system of energy production uses only carbohydrates for fuel. Whenever you begin your bout of exercise or exercise beyond your anaerobic threshold, or accelerate quickly, carbohydrates are being used with extreme inefficiency. In aerobic exercise conditions, however, fats and carbohydrates share the energy needs of the body in equal proportion, and after about an hour of moderate exercise, approximately 80% of the total energy needs come from burning fats! This has tremendous implications for the triathlete confronting the pavement for 5, 11, or even 24 hours.

To create an efficient fat-burning system, you must train continuously for long periods of time below the anaerobic threshold. This training technique allows the body to become adept at pulling triglycerides from the fat cells and processing them into usable energy. When stimulated by endurance training, the enzymes necessary for this to occur are made available in greater quantities.

The second concern, which may seem contradictory, is the evidence that fats need carbohydrates in order to be metabolized effectively. The slogan that all my exercise physiology students eventually get engrained across their frontal lobes is that "fats burn in a carbohydrate flame." When carbohydrate reserves become exhausted, the inefficient combustion of fats leaves ketone acids as an end product and can eventually create a state of ketosis. Ketosis is dangerous to the body;

it lowers the pH and causes the internal body temperature to rise. So, the next time you see a competitor jockeying for position by sprints and long accelerations, take heart: it's only a matter of time before he or she comes back to you because of a carbohydrate "burn out."

Proteins

The most important role of protein will always be to serve as the building block of the body, especially when tissue growth, turnover and/or repair are in effect. However, recent research suggests that proteins may play a greater role in the energy pool than previously thought. According to Lemon and Nagle (1981), the highly trained athlete experiences an energy-producing role from proteins. The contribution from protein breakdown can be as much as 10 to 15% of the total energy requirements for muscle contraction. This process is carried out in the liver which is capable of converting a portion of the protein chain called alanine into glucose. Reports have shown that as much as 45% of the glucose coming from the liver is produced in this way when liver glycogen stores become low.

Even though we are using proteins for energy production, the need to supplement our diets with greater amounts of proteins appears to be unnecessary. Nutritionists suggest that the average American diet contains about twice the amount of protein needed, which represents 20 to 30% of all Kcals consumed. This, coupled with the increased consumption of all foods that an athlete in training normally eats, suggests adequate quantities of protein are being consumed. However, of equal concern to protein quantity is protein quality. In order for a protein to be considered high quality, all necessary components of the protein chain, called essential amino acids, must be present and in the right proportions—a term called *biological value*. We have a food which meets these two criteria perfectly: the egg. The egg is, therefore, the standard for protein quality against which all other protein foods are compared. It is generally agreed that foods with biological values of 70% or greater are of good quality. Recognize, though, that foods with acceptable protein quality may contain only small amounts of protein. Here again, the egg is a good example; it is mainly composed of water and is only about 14% protein by weight. Therefore, a balance between protein quality and quantity must be met. Table 2.1 offers the opportunity to observe this interrelationship between protein quality and quantity among some of the more common foods.

Regardless of protein quality or quantity, if the body is lacking carbohydrates and fats, protein will be sacrificed for energy. Growth, repair, and cell turnover are all secondary priorities for protein use when energy production is not being met by other food sources. Therefore, protein is not being stored in the body, and this presents a problem. When protein is in deficit, muscle mass will be sacrificed.

I remember well an experience as a typically poor college student. I had just finished a cross-country season and had begun searching for a new challenge in sport. Being all thumbs and all feet, I decided to give weight lifting a try. Improvement came quickly, and this newly found vanity kept me coming back for

TABLE 2.1   Protein Quality and Quantity of Some Common Foods

Food	Biological Value (%)	% of Protein as Purchased
Hen's egg, whole	94	13
Cow's milk, whole	84	3.5
Fish	83	19
Beef	74	18
Soybeans	73	38
Dry beans, common	58	22
Peanuts	54	26
Green leaves	64	1.5-4.5
Yeast, brewer's	66	39
Wheat, whole grain	65	12
Wheat, white flour	52	1l
Corn, whole grain	59	10
Rice, brown	73	8
Rice, polished, white	64	7
Potato, white	67	2

Note: From FAO Nutritional Studies: *Amino Acid Content of Foods and Biological Data on Proteins.* No. 24, Rome, 1970. Reprinted with permission.

more. After about a month of regular training, my sets started dropping markedly, and my stamina had all but vanished. After another month of "much pain and no gain,"someone suggested I eat something other than pot pies and TV dinners. This suggestion solved the problem,and I learned a key lesson in sport nutrition.

Fuel Utilization in Endurance Sports

The type of fuel that meets the exercise demands depends on the type of exercise, the intensity, its duration, the level of conditioning, the environment, and the diet. These concerns are vitally important because they relate directly to efficient use of valuable energy reserves.

Exercise Intensity and Duration

We have already discussed how carbohydrates are used exclusively to fuel anaerobic exercising. Carbohydrates are also the fuel of choice when aerobic exercise is performed just under the anaerobic threshold. However, after 30 or 40 minutes of moderately intense exercise, the energy needs are shared equally by fats and carbohydrates. Fats appear to enter in as a response to the depleting carbohydrate stores in the liver and exercising muscles. As the exercise bout continues, a greater contribution is realized from the plentiful fat stores, triggering a glycogen-sparing effect. As much as 80% of the fuel demands are supplied by fats in the latter stages of long-term exercises.

Conditioning

In order for this shift in fuel usage to occur, the endurance muscles must be trained to make necessary adaptations. The endurance-trained muscles possess a greater capacity to burn fats and are capable of shifting to fat utilization earlier into the exercise. Remember that these desirable changes occur ONLY in the exercising muscles. Triathletes, therefore, must train all the muscles needed in all phases of the event in order to effectively realize this carbohydrate-sparing benefit.

Exercise Modalities

Costill (1982) presents some very relevant data concerning the type of athlete who should be concerned with the problems of glycogen depletion:

> Cyclists, marathon runners, and long distance swimmers are the athletes who must be concerned with depletion of muscle glycogen, and whom might suffer the negative effects of ill-timed sugar feedings. In our first studies on muscle glycogen depletion with distance runners, we were surprised to find that at exhaustion, there was still a reasonable amount of glycogen remaining in the thigh and calf muscles. This was in contrast with the almost complete emptying of glycogen from the thigh muscles seen in exhausted cyclists. These findings led us to assume that the determining factor for exhaustion was different for these two forms of exercise. In cycling it is possible to continue the exercise, even when the muscles are quite fatigued, but at a reduced cadence and force on the pedals. Runners, on the other hand, cannot continue beyond the fatigue point where the muscles' tension capabilities might risk literal collapse.

These observations, in light of the sequence of events in the triathlon, should serve as good advice to those who respect the need to conserve energy for the running phase.

Interrelationships of the Energy Nutrients

Some recent data we collected on triathletes illustrate the interrelationships between the two primary fuels of sport—carbohydrates (glucose) and fats (free fatty acid). In this study (Woodard & Town, 1983), five men and two women were studied during a continuous 1 mile swim (S), a 55 mile bicycle ride (B), and a 20 kilometer run (R). To avoid distorting the data, subjects were allowed to consume only water throughout the race. Figures 2.1 through 2.3 compare the blood

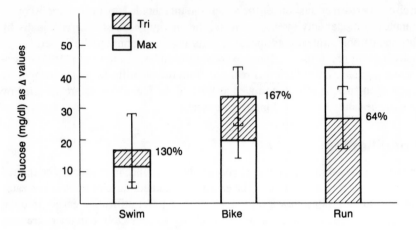

Figure 2.1 Blood glucose levels after each phase of the triathlon. Values are compared to the levels from maximal tests on respective ergometers performed while fully recovered.

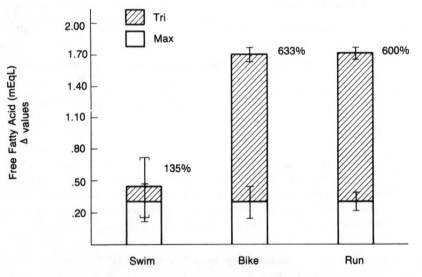

Figure 2.2 Free fatty acid levels after each phase of the triathlon. Values are compared to the levels from maximal tests on respective ergometers performed while fully recovered.

levels of glucose, free fatty acids, and lactic acid after each of the three stages of the triathlon.

Notice that after the swim event, the average blood glucose and lactic acid levels were quite high, but the free fatty acid levels were low. However, after the bicycle ride and continuing through the run phase, the exact opposite appeared.

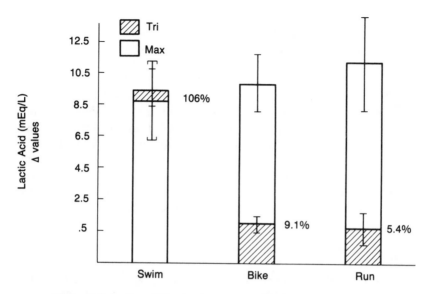

Figure 2.3 Lactic acid levels after each phase of the triathlon. Values are compared to the levels from maximal tests on respective ergometers performed while fully recovered.

Oxygen consumption data showed that the swim phase was performed at 67% of the maximal swim effort but at a maximal heart rate response. The bicycle ride was performed at 37% of the maximal bicycle effort, and the run phase was performed at 39% of maximal running effort.

The high glucose, lactic acid, and heart rate data following the swim phase, coupled with a lowered oxygen consumption value, suggest that subjects were exercising above the anaerobic threshold. The subjects had no choice but to slow down, to allow the lactic acid to clear the system, and to allow the free fatty acids to take over the energy demands. As far as performance is concerned, the "all out" swim effort forced the subjects into highly compromised bicycle and run performances.

Nonenergy Nutrients

Up to this point we have been investigating the nutrients that have caloric value. The body needs another group of nutrients with roles other than providing energy. These nutrients, like the energy nutrients, are essential to life. In this section, we will investigate three nutrients as they relate to sport performance: vitamins, minerals, and water.

Much controversy exists concerning the role vitamins and minerals play in maintaining one's health. Many advocate that these nutrients are the "cure all" for most ailments and the solution to heart disease, cancer, and the like. I sometimes feel we are still living in the days of the traveling medicine man show when people spoke of the way(s) vitamins should be used. The problem is not one of ignorance, for vitamins and minerals have been and continue to be topics of very active research. Approximately 10,000 papers are presented annually on the subjects of food and nutrition. Many of these papers represent efforts to reveal the role of vitamins and minerals and their ideal doses for our various populations. Either our researchers are failing in their efforts to bridge the gap between the laboratory and the dinner table, or the consumer's habits control his or her ability for correct decision-making processes. Despite this wealth of knowledge, the nutrition situation has changed very little in the past 10 to 20 years. At least 30% of the U.S. population have diets with inadequate nutrients, especially those of iron, calcium, vitamins A, C, and riboflavin (B_2). Malnutrition is evidenced by the physiological disorders of anemia, obesity, heart disease, hypertension, stroke, diabetes, dental disease, digestive diseases, alcoholism, and many other disorders.

Vitamins

As was stated earlier, vitamins are not food; they contribute no calories to the energy pool. People who rush out of the house with only a multiple vitamin in their stomachs have done nothing to contribute to the energy needs of their day. Vitamins carry out the important responsibility of causing a multitude of metabolic reactions to occur in the body. For instance, the many steps which take the glucose molecule and convert it into energy (ATP) are totally dependent on the availability of a variety of vitamin-related reactions.

With few exceptions, vitamins cannot be manufactured by the body and, therefore, must be supplied through our diet. What few people realize, however, is that vitamins can be used repeatedly in the various metabolic reactions. Thus, the vitamin needs of athletes are generally no greater than the requirements of sedentary people.

On the other hand, taking a multivitamin capsule containing the recommended quantity for each vitamin will not cause bodily harm. For many athletes taking a One-A-Day serves as inexpensive nutritional insurance against vitamin deficiency and might benefit the athlete psychologically if for no other reason.

Of deep concern, however, is the practice of taking megadose levels of vitamin supplements. A megadose quantity is considered to be an amount at least 10 times higher than the Recommended Dietary Allowance. Among athletes, the megadose abuse is usually from the B complex vitamins as well as vitamins C and E.

When the level of any vitamin in the body is full, the excess is either stored in the fat cells, or released from the body through urination or fecal material. Excesive amounts of some vitamins, however, function as harmful chemicals while still in the body. Excess vitamin C, for example, can raise uric acid levels in the body and eventually create gout. The body also adapts to these megadose levels by efficiently processing the excess out of the body. If someone were to suddenly return to normal vitamin consumption, a deficiency could quickly result as the body continues to clear the vitamin from its system.

Minerals

Minerals, like vitamins, also play very important roles in carrying out the many metabolic reactions in the body. The reduction of the three energy nutrients requires the involvement of many minerals, as does the building up of these small compounds into larger more complex structures. Figure 2.4 illustrates the minerals involved in the catabolism (breakdown) and anabolism (build-up) of nutrients.

Minerals are also actively involved in hormonal activity. For example, insulin needs zinc for its development, and thyroxine needs iodine. Other minerals such as calcium in bone formation and iron in red blood cell production, are necessary for cellular development.

Despite the athlete's constant need for cellular repair, exercise physiologists generally agree that for normal individuals receiving the recommended daily allowance of minerals, there is no evidence that mineral supplementation is necessary, or for that matter, that it improves performance. Like vitamins, minerals can also be used repeatedly to carry out reactions. When cells are destroyed, minerals are usually recycled before the cells' remains are voided from the body.

A possible exception to the above generalization may be worth noting to the triathlete who is involved in prolonged exercise in hot weather. The concern here

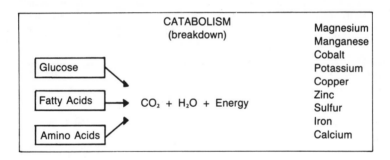

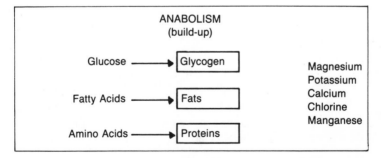

Figure 2.4 Minerals involved in the catabolism (breakdown) and anabolism (build up) of nutrients. From *Exercise Physiology: Energy, Nutrition, and Human Performance* (p. 32) by W.D. McArdle, F.I. Katch, and V.L. Katch, 1981, Philadelphia: Lea and Febiger. Reprinted by permission.

deals with the two electrolyte mineral salts (sodium and potassium chloride) that are lost through perspiration. Training and competing in hot weather can lead to excessive electrolyte losses that impair heat tolerance and exercise performance. The athlete may experience heat cramps, heat exhaustion, or heat stroke. Beware, though, that even in the extreme sweating conditions, salt supplementation should be kept at a minimum, as excess salt intake can be very dangerous. The position statement by the American College of Sports Medicine (1975) on prevention of heat injuries during distance running suggests adding only one third teaspoon of salt per liter of water. This suggestion is in drastic contrast from the days when salt tablet dispensers were in every athletic locker room.

It is rather unlikely that distance athletes will ever suffer from potassium deficiency as long as a balanced diet is consumed. But, good protection might be to eat a banana during long, hot training bouts, not only for the benefit of potassium, but for the carbohydrate content as well.

One other possible mineral deficiency that female athletes might encounter is that of iron. Because the American diet is notoriously low in iron content and because of menstruation, the female requires about twice the iron as does the male. An iron deficiency can result in a problem called iron-deficiency anemia, which would definitely impair sport performance. It is not uncommon, however, for women involved in intense endurance training to actually cease menstruating until activity levels come down. When menstruation is delayed through training, iron needs for the female are more in line with that of the male population. Like multiple vitamin supplements, mineral supplements can serve as good insurance against the concerns discussed as long as megadose quantities are not consumed.

Diet During Training

The focus of much attention in any competitive arena will inevitably be that of the training diet. As if some magic potion has been discovered, that when certain foods are consumed, increased performance is assured. One of the major promoters of unorthodox training diets is world champion triathlete Dave Scott. The readers of *Sports Illustrated* (Levin, 1983) no doubt found the champ to be not only an astonishing athlete, but an astonishing eating machine as well. The article describes Scott's meals as basically vegetarian, high in complex carbohydrates, low in fats and proteins, and each meal requiring around 1.5 hours to consume. According to Levin, "when he (Scott) was served, the scene looked like a model of the solar system; Scott was the sun, and his plates were the planets." Levin continues, "Scott's not a mere triathlete; he's a quadruple threat, if you include eating."

The main objective in setting up training diets is to assure the athlete of adequate amounts of calories through the consumption of well-balanced meals. With respect to caloric consumption, one must consider energy needs both before and after training. Caloric needs apart from those required of training vary according to one's body surface area (a relationship between height and weight), age, environment, types of food eaten, level of normal activity, and other factors. Higher caloric demands are directly associated with increased body surface area, heat and humidity, high protein diets, and more active life styles. Since the details of such a discussion are beyond the scope of this text, I refer you to the well-written and readable text *Exercise Physiology* by McArdle, Katch, and Katch (1981). Suffice it to say, that caloric demands increase as one gets taller, heavier, more active, and confronts hotter and more humid environments. Table 2.2 is an attempt to generalize over the caloric needs of men and women based on body weight and physical activity.

For the triathlete, the hours spent in training represent much greater demands and, therefore, must be added on separately. The energy expended in exercise will also fluctuate, depending on a diverse blending of variables. Not only do the above concerns directly affect caloric demands in exercise, but one must also add the factor of efficiency (both mechanical and energy utilization) to the picture. Obvious, but still worth noting, is the fact that swimmers who knife through the water, cyclists with great aerodynamics and pedal efficiency, and runners with smooth comfortable gaits will expend fewer calories than those who struggle every inch of the way. Other considerations that increase caloric demands include steeper terrains, colder and choppier water conditions, wind, and individual style of training and competition. With these limitations in mind, Table 2.3 will provide you with approximate caloric demands of the three triathlon events based on body weight and the intensity of exercise.

To demonstrate how Tables 2.2 and 2.3 are used in determining caloric needs, let us calculate how many calories I burned on October 22, 1983.—The Ironman. My race time was 10:34 and was broken down into a 1:18 swim (54 yards/min pace), 5:55 bike (19 mph pace), and 3:21 run (7.7 min/mile). My weight varied, but averaged around 170 lbs. So for the 10.5 hours of activity, my caloric expenditure would be calculated as follows:

$$78 \text{ min swim at 54 yds/min at 170 lbs} = (78 \times .070 \times 170) = 928 \text{ Kcals}$$
$$355 \text{ min bike at 19 mph at 170 lbs} = (355 \times .076 \times 170) = 4{,}611 \text{ Kcals}$$
$$201 \text{ min run at 7.7 min/mi at 170 lbs} = (201 \times .098 \times 170) = 3{,}349 \text{ Kcals}$$

TOTAL 8,888 Kcals

For the rest of the day I limped around a little, and mainly ate, so we will consider the remaining activity of the day to be "lightly active," which represents 3,500 Kcals/day for my body weight, or 1,969 Kcals for the 13½ hours left in the day. My total caloric expenditure for race day was the combination of activity (8,888) and inactivity (1,969) for a total of 10,857 Kcals. An average training day for me would more likely require around 6,000 Kcals based on my weight.

TABLE 2.2   General Caloric Needs of Men and Women

| | Activity level* | | | |
Body weight (kg)	Lightly active (kcal)	Moderately active (kcal)	Very active (kcal)	Exceptionally active (kcal)
Men				
50	2,100	2,300	2,700	3,100
55	2,310	2,530	2,970	3,410
60	2,520	2,760	3,240	3,720
65	2,700	3,000	3,500	4,000
70	2,940	3,220	3,780	4,340
75	3,150	3,450	4,040	4,650
80	3,360	3,680	4,320	4,960

*The activity levels defined by FAO/WHO are as follows:

LIGHTLY ACTIVE

Men: most professional men (lawyers, doctors, accountants, teachers, architects, etc.), office workers, shop workers, unemployed men

Women: housewives in houses with mechanical household appliances, office workers, teachers, most professional women

MODERATELY ACTIVE

Men: most men in light industry, students, building workers (excluding heavy laborers), many farmworkers, soldiers not in active service, fishermen

Women: most women in light industry, housewives without mechanical household appliances, students, department store workers

Note: From FAO/WHO: Energy and Protein Requirements, *WHO Technical Report* No. 522; FAO Nutrition Report No. 52 Geneva and Rome, 1973, pp. 25 and 31. Reprinted with permission.

Regardless of the numbers calculated for yourself, you must next consider a more pleasant problem: how to consume these large amounts of calories. The Dave Scott eating workout is certainly a nutritionally sound program. Low-fat, low-protein, high-complex carbohydrate vegetarian diets will certainly aid in the prevention of heart disease and hypertension to name a few. There is no argument that complex carbohydrate foods are the best way to ingest the all-important sugars as well. And, if you are a fully sponsored triathlete like the champ, you will no doubt be able to afford the time and money required of such a diet.

Few of us will ever be prepared to enter into this "heavenly bliss" of a diet. So let us take a more realistic perspective toward the triathletes' diet. According to the American Dietetic Association and the American Diabetes Association, the ideal diet should consist of approximately 12 to 15% of the Kcals coming from protein, 20 to 25% of the Kcals coming from fat, and the remaining Kcals from carbohydrates. The best carbohydrate calories should be of the complex type (starches) instead of the simple carbohydrates (sugars). Fats should be poly-

TABLE 2.2   CONT.

		Activity level*		
Body weight (kg)	Lightly active (kcal)	Moderately active (kcal)	Very active (kcal)	Exceptionally active kcal)
Women				
40	1,440	1,600	1,880	2,200
45	1,620	1,800	2,120	2,480
50	1,800	2,000	2,350	2,750
55	2,000	2,200	2,600	3,000
60	2,160	2,400	2,820	3,300
65	2,340	2,600	3,055	3,575
70	2,520	2,800	3,290	3,850

VERY ACTIVE

Men: some agricultral workers, unskilled laborers, forestry workers, army recruits and soldiers in active service, mineworkers, steelworkers

Women: some farmworkers (especially in peasant agriculture), dancers, athletes

EXCEPTIONALLY ACTIVE

Men: lumberjacks, blacksmiths, rickshaw pullers

Women: construction workers

unsaturated (oils) instead of the saturated type (solids). Proteins must be attained from a variety of foods in efforts to attain the necessary mix of essential amino acids. The ADA also promotes eating three meals/day with the calories equally distributed between meals. I strongly suggest eating in accordance with these guidelines as often as possible.

However, I still find these guidelines, like Scott's, unrealistic. Consider first the need to consume 5,000 Kcals in one day. Complex carbohydrates should represent approximately 60 to 65% of the total calories, which is about 3,250 Kcals. If one is to stick to consuming complex carbohydrates (fruits are not of this category), this figure represents 7.5 lbs of potatoes or 58 slices of bread! Adding to this theoretical diet would be 20 to 25% of the Kcals coming from fats with the emphasis being on foods high in polyunsaturates and low in cholesterol. A 1000 Kcals of margarine, for example, could be used on the bread or potatoes, but this represents only about one-third pound of margarine. On the other hand, you could spend the fat calories by frying your potatoes in 4 oz. of corn oil. Proteins should represent 12 to 15% of the calories, or around 750 Kcals. Because these should come from a mix of sources, a lettuce salad containing sesame seeds, cheese, soybeans, and egg whites would represent the preferred choice. Be conservative here because your potatoes and breads also contain calories in the form of protein.

TABLE 2.3   Caloric Demands of the Triathlon Events

Activity	Intensity	Kcal/Lb/min
Swimming (crawl)	20 yds/min	.032
	45 yds/min	.058
	50 yds/min	.070
Bicycling	13 mph	.045
	15 mph	.049
	17 mph	.057
	19 mph	.076
	21 mph	.090
	23 mph	.109
	25 mph	.139
Running	11:30 min/mi - 5.2 mph	.061
	9:00 min/mi - 6.7 mph	.088
	8:00 min/mi - 7.5 mph	.094
	7:00 min/mi - 9.0 mph	.103
	6:00 min/mi -10.0 mph	.114
	5:30 min/mi -11.0 mph	.131

Note: Data compiled from Cundiff, 1979, McCardle, 1981, & Whitt, 1983.

This ludicrous example is an attempt to put the training diet into a more realistic perspective. My main objection to this type of diet is not over the issue of fats and proteins but with the unrealistic grudge against simple carbohydrates. Granted, simple sugars can cause havoc with your body when used in great quantities for long periods of time. I am soberly reminded of heart disease, of diabetes, and of obesity which can all be traced in part to high sugar consumption. Nevertheless, we cannot disregard the importance of consuming simple sugars as they relate to the nutritional needs of the triathlete, (for instance, the speed at which simple sugars enter the bloodstream, ready to serve the starving, glycogen-depleted cells). Consider also, the high caloric content which our sugar-based foods contain. I, for one, prefer to limit the food that I must carry and consume in both training and in competition which is best accomplished through consuming sugar-based foods. Finally, on a more psychological or mental stability perspective, consider the need to satisfy one's taste for sweets.

With only 8 miles to the finish of my Ironman experience, I vividly remember feeling myself hitting the wall. For the next two aid stations, I drank a full cup of Coke, and within minutes, I was back on pace without any more dizziness or mental dysfunction for the rest of the race. Finally, if another reason is necessary for having sugars as a part of your training diet, consider what poor choices you have at the races' aid stations for complex carbohydrates. At Ironman, the only choice would have been the bread component of the guava jam sandwiches. Simple sugars, on the other hand, were readily available in the form of orange sections, bananas, cookies, Gatorade, and Coke. Based on these aforementioned reasons, I could no more think of training without ice cream in the freezer, Coke, and fresh fruits in the cooler, and cookies in the cupboard, than I would of riding without derailleurs on my bike.

A word of caution, however: Consuming sugar-based foods should always be done in small quantities and at dispersed intervals. When you flood your system with sugars, insulin is recruited in great quantities to clear sugars from the bloodstream. Not only does this play havoc with your blood sugar levels, but it also fatigues the insulin-producing cells of the pancreas which can eventually destroy these cells—a condition we know as diabetes.

Diet and Exercise Recovery

One of the most overlooked concerns related to nutrition and exercise is the role of diet as it contributes to exercise recovery. Triathletes are often working out twice a day, which leaves the body in a continuous state of repair, needing to resupply its energy stores. The type of diet, the amount eaten, and even the delay in which food is eaten after exercise can play an important role in effective recovery efforts. Hultman and Bergstrom (1967) and Piehl (1974) exercised subjects for 1 hour by swimming, running, or bicycling and 1 additional hour of heavier, exhausting exercise. These subjects then ate one of three diets: either a high carbohydrate diet, a fat and protein diet, or no food at all. Figure 2.5 shows the

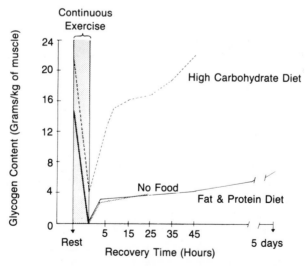

Figure 2.5 Rate and level of glycogen return in response to three different training diets. From *The Physiological Basis of Physical Education and Athletics*, 3rd edition (p. 39) by E.L. Fox and D.K. Mathews, 1981, Philadelphia: Saunders College Publishing. Reprinted by permission.

rate of glycogen return into the exhausted muscle under the three different diet conditions.

Note that the no-food diet and the fat and protein diet allowed for only an insignificant amount of glycogen resynthesis even after 5 days into recovery. The high-carbohydrate diet, on the other hand, allowed for replenishment to the point of 60% completion after 10 hours and total return after 46 hours. When carbohydrate replenishment is incomplete between workouts, the workouts that follow will inevitably be shorter, less intense, and more prone to injury.

Recovery time is also necessary for rebuilding the microstructural tissue breakdown in muscle. This effectively occurs only when protein is available to create a rebuilding environment. However, in a diet where carbohydrates are unavailable, proteins are diverted from their normal tasks and are used to contribute to the energy production pool. Repair under these conditions must wait.

Chapter 3

The Psychology of Performance

Up to this point we have investigated sport performance from physiological and nutritional perspectives. For various reasons, most writers choose to limit their writings on sport performance to these two major areas. One major reason is that physiological and nutritional data as it relates to sport can be easily measured. Terms such as calories consumed, oxygen consumption, lactic acid, interval splits, and elapsed time over specific distances are all ways we can describe sport performance. We have been measuring performance from a physiological perspective for a long time; hence, the biology-based sport sciences are currently enjoying a wave of popularity.

We all acknowledge that success in sport requires more than a finely tuned, carbohydrate-loaded body, for popular chatter around the finish line includes expressions such as "psyched out," "felt heavy," "choked," and so on. And for those who performed up to their expectations, comments such as "felt strong" and "got psyched" indicate the total person performed at optimum.

Compared to the physiological study of sport, the psychological study is relatively new and undeveloped. Sport psychologists are making rapid progress in developing techniques to identify and quantify the mental traits conducive to successful sport performance. But these experts are battling against some great inconsistencies. Let me illustrate by using the typical inverted "U" which describes the relationship between motivation and sport performance.

Most people agree that we need motivation in order to perform at optimal levels, and they are equally aware that if we are overly motivated, sport performance will be compromised. So, we simply seek out, through trial and error, the optimal level of motivation.

This discussion is not nearly so simple; the level of motivation requires adjustments based on a variety of confounding variables. Figure 3.1 also compares levels of motivation to task complexity. When the task is complex in nature, the level of motivation needs to be less than when it is compared with more simple tasks. Professional golfers are well aware of this problem and serve as good examples by trying to stay cool and calm.

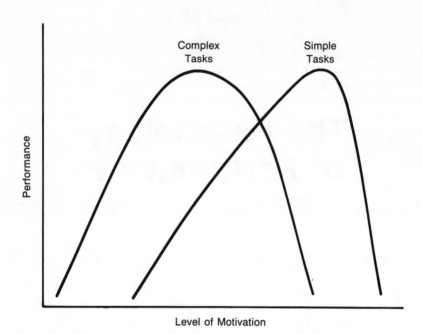

Figure 3.1 Relationship of performance to level of motivation.

An even bigger problem affecting the curves in Figure 3.1 is measurement error and individual differences. Each person contributing to the data pool will add two error factors to the data. First, we are humans, and since no two humans are identical, our data will naturally differ between individuals even when efforts to control these differences are extensively carried out. Second, researchers measure with imprecise instruments. As time goes on, measurement error will reduce because of technological advances; but problems of sensitivity, reliability, and repeatability will continue to plague data accuracy. Therefore, psychological data collection will always be difficult to quantify. (Wouldn't it be nice if the mind was studied as easily as the rest of the body?)

Physiologically, one can say that the higher the maximum oxygen consumption, the greater success the athlete can expect to experience in middle distance sports. Tossing out psychological generalities with the same level of confidence would only demonstrate naiveté or ignorance.

Now that the problems of sport psychology have been introduced, I would like to present the more accepted data that relates to sport performance with special attention given to endurance sport performance.

Motivation to Train and to Compete

A logical beginning for our investigation would be to study the reasons why people gravitate toward a sport that requires great sacrifices but offers such small measurable rewards. In tracing the roots of the triathlon, we find its beginnings were developed in the typical fashion of most "irrational" endurance contests. The setting was, of course, a barroom in Hawaii and the topic, no doubt, was physical prowess. Since physical prowess has never been categorized according to sport difficulty, perspectives must have differed to the point where an impasse developed between three major endurance sports—swimming, cycling, and running. Surely, the suds were flowing freely as were the half-baked solutions. The impasse was broken, and the solution surfaced like bubbles in their beer. The answer—combining three well-known Hawaiian endurance events—the Waikiki Rough Water Swim, the 112-mile bike race around Oahu, and the Honolulu Marathon to be run in continuous fashion. The first to finish was expected to be the one whose main sport carried the greatest influence—a logical assumption if in an intoxicated state. So, before these men had time to return to their senses, the bet was on, and macho men never back down from bets!

It's doubtful that many other triathletes found their way into the sport through similar predicaments, but for our participation, all have reasons which are difficult to explain. For most, the motive(s) to train and to compete is highly internalized. Unlike tennis, golf, basketball, baseball, and football, the triathlon carries little external reward. I doubt the highest paid athlete will ever be a triathlete, appear on the front of a Wheaties box, or ever become a household word. If your romance with the triathlon includes these motives, I suggest you honeymoon in a different sport.

What really motivates a triathlete? Motive, according to Birch and Veroff (1966), is the strength of attraction or repulsion to a general class of consequences. Alderman (1974) broadens the definition by describing motivation as the general level of arousal to action in an individual. The motives, then, become the specific conditions attached to particular courses of action and to the consequences that result from the arousal. Motives by these definitions may sound like impulses, but they are different; motives are more latent and relatively stable dispositions.

Realize, also, that motivation includes the will to avoid as well as the will to engage. When training in a multiphasic sport, both the motive "to do" and the motive "not to do" can be working simultaneously. (More on this problem later.)

The common thread that unites all rational-thinking humans is the need to achieve. Deep within all of us is the motive to attain some internally defined standard of excellence, whether through sport, profession, family, hobby, or whatever. This achievement motivation is often carried out by pitting oneself against some other person or persons, but this drive can also be fulfilled by competing against a set of personal standards. Thus, this standard of excellence can be internalized (one's personal level of aspiration) or externalized (achievement through competing against other people). Either way, it is important to understand that an individual's effort to constantly achieve certain goals in life is a fundamental aspect of personality and humanity. When the basic human need to achieve is ever present, triathletes are no different than anyone else. We all know what the mountain climber means when asked why he climbs: the common response, "because it is there,'' wells up in each one of us, only in different ways and at different levels of intensity.

Then why are people attracted to the triathlon as their personal ''mountain''? Surely satisfaction and personal achievement can be attained by less demanding means. Why, for instance, would a world class cyclist like John Howard enter the unfamiliar territory of triathlon competition when his reputation as a cyclist is well established? Or why do so many professionals, successful businessmen, and even you yourself (who have probably achieved high levels of success in other areas in the past), confront this sporting monster called the triathlon? This question can be answered from two different perspectives.

First, the triathlete is challenged by tasks possessing intermediate levels of difficulty. Researchers classify achievers into two different categories: those who choose tasks of intermediate difficulty, and those who choose either difficult or simple tasks. Individuals who are high achievers tend to perform successfully at any task they attempt; thus they are not attracted to tasks involving a high possibility of failure, nor are they likely to choose tasks that are ridiculously easy, for there is no satisfaction in doing something everyone can do. Consequently, the high achiever gravitates toward challenges of intermediate difficulty. On the other hand, those less motivated, realizing that failure is highly probable for all who attempt, will choose tasks that are unrealistically difficult; therefore, failure is expected and success is given over to chance. Both achievers have a place in sport and business. After all, few football coaches and fans are likely to use a quarterback who is not willing to take chances, but who is comfortable only when plays develop as planned.

The dynamics of the triathlon suit the high achiever perfectly. The three events—swim, bike, and run—are within the capabilities of us all. Efficiency in each sport is associated mainly with consistent training and with only a moderate reliance on technique.

Given adequate training time, some good equipment, and hopefully injury-free miles, the goal of finishing a triathlon is well within reach. Surprised to find so many successful businessmen and professionals taking on the triathlon challenge? To me, the challenge fits the personality perfectly.

The challenge to simply finish (the mountain climber rationale) is the second possibility why people are attracted to the triathlon. History will support the fact that Americans have always been attracted to novel ideas. Back in the early 1970s, completing a marathon run was a significant and prestigious accomplishment for the highly talented runner. However, with the popularity of aerobic exercise and the advancements in the running shoe design, the marathon descended onto the masses.

I can remember traveling a full day in 1972 to compete in my first marathon. At the starting line, I was joined by 160 others like me who had traveled long distances to find a marathon challenge. My finish time of 3:02 was good enough for 21st place and for a hero's welcome at my college campus. Times certainly have changed.

Today, the marathon no longer carries the aura it once did. Marathons are big business, attracting thousands of competitors of all abilities. Finishing the footrace is still a tremendous accomplishment, and the event will undoubtedly remain a popular challenge for many. The novelty of the marathon, however, has run its course. The masses have conquered the distance, and the endurance athlete is looking for new boundaries to surpass.

Finishing a triathlon is still a unique accomplishment. Very few have conquered the triathlon, and in coffee breaks everywhere, people are still buzzing over this new challenge. Presently, the triathlon is novel and that makes it very attractive.

Personality Qualities of the Triathlete

We all have associated with people who seemed to lack the "right stuff" for athletics, falling short in our expectations of proper size, speed, and so on, to be successful. But much to our surprise, these individuals have somehow overcome those perceived limitations and demonstrated performance at a high level. These people are overachievers. On the other hand, we have also known people who seemed to have all it takes and more, but have fallen short of our expectations. Because we are a psychobiological organism, our mental or psychological state has much to do with our physiological performance. This section presents some data investigating the mental disposition of successful athletes and applies these data to the triathlete.

Attraction Versus Withdrawal

As mentioned earlier, one of the biggest problems with psychological research is individual differences. In reality, the inverted "U" graph previously discussed would be shaped differently for each individual measured. Duffy (1949, 1951, 1962) attempts to list the factors which vary between individuals' internal motivation as follows:

1. Fatigue
2. Stimulants or sedatives
3. General changes in fitness
4. Changes in the activity in which one is engaged
5. Variations in one's interpretation of the demands of the situation

Duffy generalizes that the competitive demands of a particular sport will inherently raise the individual's level of motivation. This rise can affect a person's level of arousal, both in its direction and in its intensity. In some cases, the level of arousal will be too high, and the response becomes one of avoiding the competitive situation.

Duffy's observations have significant implications for the triple-sport competitor. Many athletes enter triathlon training and competition with strengths in only one or two of the three events; and because training where one's strengths lie is more gratifying, the area(s) of weakness tend to be avoided. Once placed in a competitive situation in the weak areas of competancy, the withdrawal response is further magnified.

Suppose, for example, the USTS (United States Triathlon Series) comes to your area, and you realize that you could easily bike 40K and run 10K, but the 1.5K swim is not your strong event. In training, you eventually work up to swimming 1.5K in either the local pool or nearby lake. Your confidence in swimming is adequate but highly conditional. On race day, your objective is merely to endure the 1.5K swim and then develop your impressive comeback in the bike and run stages.

Race day arrives and some unexpected complications develop, something you failed to consider during your training. Examples may include the stark reality of 800 other competitors vying for limited water space. The crowded conditions interrupt your stroke rhythm, and you are even forced to readjust your goggles which were jarred by another struggling competitor. Added to the unexpected might be the need to cover extra distances because of veering off course. Anxiety increases, stroke efficiency decreases. Thoughts of surviving the ordeal suddenly become a higher priority than competing. You, therefore, find yourself struggling, falling back. More people start to swim up your back because of your slowed pace—greater anxiety. The cycle continues. What an ordeal!

Finally, after what seemed to be an hour of battle, the water's bottom appears through your goggles—you've made it. Now off to cycling and running—more familiar environments.

Now you realize that the problem becomes much greater than simply "enduring" the swim. The fatigue and added anxiety from the swim will carry over into the two other events, which will surely create compromised performance throughout the rest of the race.

In light of Duffy's motivational factors, I suggest that triathletes focus their competitive behavior toward viewing the triathlon as a complete package. Avoiding specific areas of the triple-sport event and strengthening others is an irrational approach which will inevitably lead to disappointing performance and avoidance in the future. Focus your objectives on the larger picture—the end-product resulting from performing well in all three events: Where you have strengths, maintain; where you have weaknesses, confront with a finish line motivation. Realize that everyone has the tendency to avoid, but the more you confront the weaker areas, the more avoidance behavior diminishes.

Mood States

Sports psychologists who actively research the mind and sport performance universally arrive at one consistent observation: Successful athletes, in all sports, possess superior mental and emotional health. Successful athletes consistently show fewer signs of psychopathology (mental illness) and lower levels of anxiety, neuroticism, and depression than less successful athletes, as well as the general population (Morgan, 1980).

Sports psychologist Bill Morgan (1979) compared world class athletes to average-fit college students in six different categories of "mood states." Figure 3.2 shows the typical iceberg-shaped curve given by world class athletes as adjusted to the straight line college students' scores (shown as the T score of 50).

Athletes score below the college age norms in the mood states of anxiety, depression, anger, psychic fatigue, and confusion, but score considerably higher in psychic vigor.

Morgan has researched several athletic populations in an attempt to predict which ones will attain high levels of success (make the team) and which ones will not (cut from the team). A Profile of Mood States (POMS) is administered at the onset of training camp, and then the level of individual success is observed at the end of training camp. Figure 3.3 portrays the "iceberg" profiles of wrestlers who made the 1972 U.S. Olympic Team and of those who were cut.

Of the 40 candidates, 10 wrestlers were selected to compete: of the 10 selected, 9 were predicted by the results of the POMS test to make the team.

These results gained tremendous notoriety, and coaches from other sports began to express interest in this important tool. Using the same investigative methodology, Morgan and Johnson (1978) studied olympic oarsmen and 24 of the country's top marathoners and middle-distance runners (Morgan and Pollock,

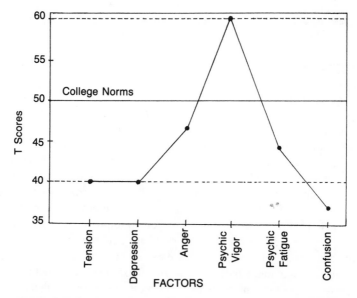

Figure 3.2 Typical iceberg profile of mood states characterizing world class athletes as compared to college norms. From "Prediction of performance in athletics" in P. Klavor (Ed.), *Proceedings of the Applied Sciences Symposium of the Canadian Society for Psychomotor Learning and Sport Psychology Congress*, 1979, Toronto.

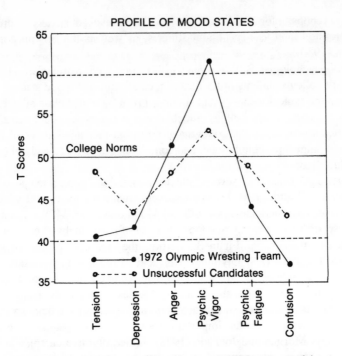

Figure 3.3 Psychological profiles of successful and unsuccessful candidates for the U.S. Olympic Wrestling team. From "The iceberg profile" by W.P. Morgan, July 1980, *Psychology Today*, p. 97. Copyright 1980 by *Psychology Today*. Reprinted by permission.

1977). Figure 3.4 compares the POMS profiles of the successful competitors in the three different sports.

Although the ingredients that enter into these three sports are much different physiologically, the psychology, at least from a mood state perspective, is very similar. All three athletic populations scored "below the surface" on tension, depression, fatigue, and confusion, but significantly "above the surface" on vigor.

An argument has been raised whether sport participation creates the appearance of the profile shown, or whether successful athletes bring this profile into their sport. Most likely both occur simultaneously. What might arise as a more important question is how to alter one's mental and physical environment to create a more desirable profile. Probably the best effort to improve one's psychological profile would be to reduce or resolve the problems irrelevant to the task at hand. Most elite athletes are elite because they expend very little energy toward concerns outside of their immediate sport world. Sponsorships allow these people to dedicate their days to training and to use the best equipment. With this in mind, it is easy to see how successful athletes can maintain a low level of tension, depression, and confusion. Most of us will never enjoy such freedom and must be content to work our training programs in and around other responsibilities.

What we can do, however, is to set realistic goals for ourselves—goals that are relative to our other commitments. We can also attempt to eliminate areas in our lives that create tension, depression, anger, and confusion. Finally, we can attempt to reprioritize our commitments, at least temporarily, in efforts to better focus our attention on the task at hand.

Because we have no data to describe the "iceberg" profile of triathletes, we can only speculate. Obviously, the nature of our event would require mood levels that are similar to what we see coming from elite athletes. However, because of the added hours required to train for three events, I expect triathletes would score even lower than elite athletes in the areas of anxiety, anger, and psychic fatigue. I would attempt to combine these three mood states and categorize them under the name of "patience." Patience is probably the greatest pyschological virtue the triathlete can bring into the sport. How easy it is to get caught up in the race and find yourself overextended in one event; or how easy it is to get irritated when other swimmers inadvertently interrupt your stroke. I have personally been slugged by a competitor, who out of frustration, probably felt that colliding while swimming was a competitive technique. How easy it would be to drop out because of a flat tire when the 2 minutes needed to change it would seldom affect your standing in even some of the biggest triathlons in the country!

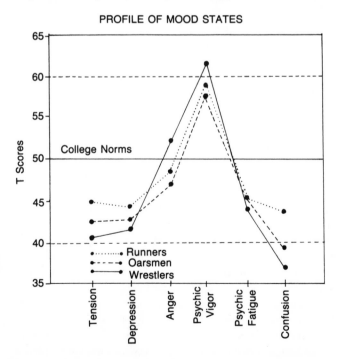

Figure 3.4. Psychological profiles of world class runners, oarsmen, and wrestlers. From "The iceberg profile" by W.P. Morgan, July 1980, *Psychology Today*, p. 102. Copyright 1980 by *Psychology Today*. Reprinted by permission.

No, the triathlete needs to exercise a surplus of patience—a must if one expects to perform at optimum.

Morgan's studies of mood states carry additional information worth noting. For instance, the profile of mood states (POMS) changes during the different phases of the competitive seasons and may serve to screen for individuals who are getting stale. Staleness can result from mental and/or physical overtraining or from maintaining peak performance for too long.

Finally, and perhaps most importantly, Morgan's work reveals the complex interrelationships that moods play in successful sport performance. If tests are administered to get at the psychological potential of the athlete, the results should never be taken out of context. We must also assess the physiological and biomechanical contributions that each individual possesses.

Chapter 4

Setting Up
Your Training Camp

Sport scientists are constantly trying to generate the ultimate formula which will accurately predict success in sport. Exercise physiologists make their predictions based on muscle fiber type, maximum oxygen consumption, anaerobic threshold, and other factors. The sport psychologists are quantifying each athlete's level of anxiety, depression, anger, extroversion, and mental fatigue to create their profiles. The kinesiologists examine concerns such as stride length, cadence, force, and velocity to create their "reference athlete." Even if sport scientists are successful in defining the perfect prescription for success in any given sport, I am still convinced that the formula's application will be met with great difficulty, for the athlete is far more complex than the sensitivity of any formula.

We can all think of sport personalities who rise to the top, but technically speaking, they fall short by "ideal" physical standards. Many have overcome the limitations of being too tall, too short, too slow, or too heavy by capitalizing on some of their other virtues. Regardless of all the virtues one brings into sport, including all the "natural" ability possible, there is simply no substitute for hard, consistent, disciplined training! Athletes whose movements look like poetry in motion on the field have spent countless hours developing their skill and stamina one rhyme at a time.

This chapter presents research-based ideas which will facilitate the development of your triathlon training camp. Each of you possesses a unique set of training strengths and limitations. Some have a high threshold of pain and the perseverance to tolerate a megamileage training program. Some have limited time constraints but possess refined movement mechanics. The combination of personal strengths and weaknesses are as varied as the number of participants. Because each of you enters into the triathlon with a unique set of qualities, I feel compelled to direct you toward your training regimen, not to create one.

Isn't it interesting to read the various success formulas of premier triathletes and their advice to the public? While one promotes daily stints of near Ironman distances in all three sports, another promotes short, high-intensity training as

TABLE 4.1   Final Performance

Fitness Traits	Skill Traits	Physical Traits	Psychological Traits
Aerobic endurance	Swim mechanics	Physique	Achievement
Swimming	Bike mechanics	Height	Aggression
Bicycling	Run mechanics	Weight	Affiliation
Running	Kinesthesis	Body fat	Independence
Transition efficiency		Heat tolerance	Desire to excel
		Cold tolerance	Desire to win
			Determination
			Patience
			Emotional stability
			Pain tolerance

the quickest way to the finish line. We are indeed grateful for all the insight that results from those dedicated athletes who repeatedly win. But to emulate anyone's training program based on another's personal success violates an understanding of our uniqueness: We are not clones.

Table 4.1 categorizes the various dimensions in the triathlon that culminate into the final performance. As you review these dimensions, rate yourself among the various traits listed.

In addition to the physical and emotional traits that you bring into the triathlon, the pragmatic concerns such as your calendar, finances, family, and social life, also need to be considered. With these underlying traits and concerns in mind, let us first investigate the basic principles of endurance training and then make application to the triathlon.

The Principles of Training

In order to maximize your training program, you must adhere to three training principles. These principles are the overload principle, progression, and specificity of training.

Overload Principle

If you were to enter a "pain-free" sit-up program, the plan would be to perform sit-ups only to the point where you feel the slightest sensation of fatigue. Rest assured, you will most likely experience injury free-exercising, but you would have violated the overload principle. The body adapts to the demands that are placed on it. If the body, in its current state, can accomplish the tasks set before it, then no adaptations are necessary. In order to experience improved sit-up performance, for example, the effort must exceed the demands to which the body is accustomed.

The demands placed on your body, in any exercise, must be of sufficient intensity to encourage metabolic adaptations, but not at intensities so great that illness, injury, and overtraining become a high risk. Appropriate doses of speed and distance in each event, therefore, must be established and revised continually based on your current level of fitness.

Progression

The principle of progression introduces the idea that training should proceed at exercise doses that continually increase as the body adapts. Without the ability to quantify your workouts, there is no way of knowing if your training regime is working.

Progression must be observed in two levels. Level 1 is the initiation phase, characterized by the trauma your body undergoes anytime you begin a new exercise program. The body goes through a period of stiffness and soreness, but even the bones and joints are adapting in efforts to accommodate your new physical lifestyle. The initiation phase takes time to complete, and exercise should be performed moderately with generous rest periods. Limit your workouts to 3 or 4 days per week with each exercise bout lasting between 20 and 45 minutes.

After 3 to 4 weeks in the initiation phase, you will establish a proper base; your body will have made many adjustments and should no longer experience the trauma it did in the beginning. Level 2 progression can now be incorporated from this established base. In this level of progression may be called *sensible aggression,* you push yourself aggressively, at the same time you are remaining sensitive to any warning signs your body might be giving. Some of these warning signs might include:

chest pains
light headedness
dizziness
nausea
extreme difficulty in breathing
extreme fatigue
sudden loss of skin color
joint inflammation or joint soreness
muscle soreness that persists through recovery

Many athletes are serious about their training; they have realistic and opportunistic goals but do not approach their training aggressively. If you enter any workout without the intent to be better conditioned than before you started the workout, then you're better off to let the training session pass. *Training at mediocrity will often breed competing at mediocrity.*

Specificity of Training

Specificity of training implies that sport movements are specific and that training in one sport does not improve performance in other sports. Shocked? This, contrary to opinion, is true. Many studies have been done where untrained individuals have been trained by either running, swimming, or bicycling, but tested before and after training on a variety of exercise environments. Magel and co-workers (1974) trained college-aged males by swimming, then tested them before and after training by both treadmill running and tethered swimming. Swim training resulted in increased swimming oxygen consumption at maximum effort, whereas small, nonsignificant improvements were noted when pre- and posttreadmill tests were compared.

McArdle and others (1978) used the same procedures but with running as the only training modality. Following training, maximal efforts showed an increase of 6% and 2.6% in oxygen consumption in treadmill and swimming tests, respectively.

In another significant study, Stromme, Ingjer, and Meen (1977) tested the maximum aerobic power of 14 female and 10 male competitive cross-country skiers, 8 male rowers, and 5 male cyclists. Subjects were exercised to maximum by uphill running and on their sport specific ergometer. All groups showed the highest maximum oxygen consumption values while being tested on their sport specific modality. For the skiers, uphill skiing resulted in a 3% greater oxygen consumption value than uphill running. The rowers were 4.2% higher when rowing over uphill running, and the cyclists were 5.6% greater when biking compared to uphill running.

Contrary to the concept of specificity of exercise, some cardiovascular "carry-over" appears when subjects are trained on a running program but are tested under a variety of exercise conditions. Carry-over has been demonstrated from run training when tested on the bicycle ergometer (Town & Sinning, 1982; Pechar et al. 1974; Roberts & Alspaugh, 1972), load carrying tasks, and even arm-cranking skills (Van Handel et al., 1976).

Let's take the specificity of training concept one step further. Training at one speed within a sport does not necessarily offer you the greatest improvement when you compete at a different speed. Figure 4.1 silhouettes the running form of an elite-class middle-distance runner who we filmed while running on a treadmill at 6, 8, 10, and 12 mph (Town, 1982).

Note, at slower speeds, the body is comparably more upright, stride length and stride rate being shorter and smaller. As the speeds increase, more forward lean is realized, but with concomitant increases in stride length and rate. This suggests that at different running speeds, the body takes on a different running form. With each speed, new muscles are being used, and even the same muscles are used differently. What this says to the triathlete (where efficiency is paramount in importance) is that you should replicate as closely as possible the speeds you intend to use in each event on the day of competition. What better way to

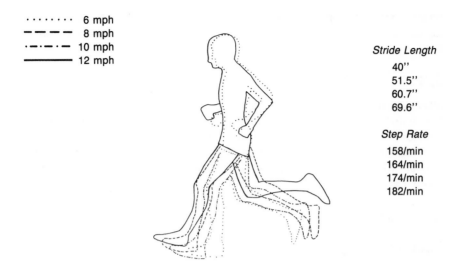

········ 6 mph
− − − − 8 mph
·—·—·— 10 mph
———— 12 mph

Stride Length

40"
51.5"
60.7"
69.6"

Step Rate
158/min
164/min
174/min
182/min

Figure 4.1 Superimposed running forms at 6, 8, 10, and 12 mph.

create the most efficient swimming, cycling, and running form than to train at the exact speed you intend to use in competition?

Aerobic Training Programs

Because the triathlon places such high demands on the aerobic energy system, I will limit the types of training methods to those that incorporate work efforts longer than 1 to 2 minutes. Efforts requiring less than this time frame do not really enhance the aerobic system, rather they overload the lactic acid/anaerobic system.

Long Slow Distance (LSD) Training

This type of program suggests that training intensity is less than the competition pace (60 to 80% of the maximum heart rate), but at greater distances than the competition demands. Some proponents of LSD view its use as a way to establish a conditioning base from which to build onto with the necessary speed. Others suggest LSD as being the total program with speed as a natural outcome from the training.

Short Rest Interval Training

Training in this way consists of work intervals lasting around 2 minutes with recovery times between work intervals lasting a minute or less. Because recovery is never complete, the aerobic system is enhanced. An average swimmer, for example, might perform 10 repeat 100 meter intervals in 1 minute send-offs. If the swimmer completes the work in 90 seconds, then the swimmer uses a 30-second rest interval.

Speed Play (Fartlek)

Bikers and runners are often attracted to this training technique, but even swimmers utilize speed play. Speed play involves informal bouts of fast and slow intensities at varying intervals of work and recovery. The slow intensities serve as an incomplete recovery effort. Often, the format is spontaneous and performed over unmarked terrain such as through forests, golf courses, or over country roads. Speed play training enhances both the aerobic and anaerobic capacities and also increases one's speed. Because of its rather impromptu format, speed play is a relatively nonquantifiable training technique which many consider a shortcoming.

Pace Training

Although this concept as a training technique is relatively unknown, it has great application to the triathlete. Simply stated, pace training is an effort to closely replicate the actual competition environment. The speed which you intend to use in competition would be replicated in your training program. By design, the pace you choose, if realistic, would be reasonably maintained in each workout, continuing until your conditioning allows you to extend the training work bouts to the actual competition distances. To carry the concept even further, the terrain and environmental factors (heat, wind, humidity, hills) should also be mirrored as closely as possible.

The major criticism of pace training is that you can "burn out" when this technique becomes the main training diet, and in sports where speed is extremely intense, the criticism is justified. Because the triathlon involves three different events, each requires shared interest in the total energy pool. By necessity then, all events are performed at high, but submaximal intensities. Therefore, in the context of the triathlon, burnout is much less of a concern because the pace is less than maximum intensity; yet at the same time, it is performed at race pace.

Table 4.2 categorizes these four training techniques according to their aerobic and anaerobic enhancement.

Aerobic Conditioning Programs Compared

In deciding which type of training program to use during the various phases of training, you must first have a final training objective in mind. For example, do you want to maximize your aerobic power, your anaerobic power, or maximize efficiency? A classic study of elite distance runners done by Costill, Fink, and Pollock (1976) might offer important direction in deciding which training program to use. The authors miraculously gathered 14 of the top distance runners

TABLE 4.2   Aerobic Training Methods and the Approximate Development Percentages of the Various Energy Systems

	Development (Percent)		
Training Method	Speed (ATP-CP)	Aerobic System (Oxygen)	Anaerobic System (Lactic Acid)
Long Slow Distance	2	93	5
Pace Training	10	60	30
Short Rest Interval	30	20	50
Speed Play (Fartlek)	20	40	40

of the time and performed every metabolic test imaginable in an effort to discover what makes the elite distance runner elite. The roster of competitors read like the academy awards in distance running: Prefontaine, Kardong, Moore, Shorter, Galloway, and Tuttle. Let's look at their maximum oxygen consumption values. The average maximum oxygen consumption values for the group was 77.4 ml/kg/min, with a range of 71.3 to 84.4 ml/kg/min. Among the group were six runners with marathon times faster than 2:20. Averaging the maximum oxygen consumption values of these six, the value drops to 74.3 ml/kg/min with a range of 71.3 to 76.9. In other words, all the elite marathoners pulled down the average maximum oxygen consumption. The authors defend this seemingly dichotomous observation with the following statement:

> Shorter's maximum oxygen consumption value of 71.3 ml/kg/min is far from exceptional for an endurance athlete. Although this value is well below what might be anticipated for one of the world's best marathon runners, it is not unlike the value reported for Derek Clayton, holder of the world's best marathon performance (2 hr, 8 min, 22 sec). Despite his ability to run at an average speed of 4 min, 54 sec/mile for 30 min with little blood lactate accumulation, Clayton's maximum oxygen consumption was only 69.7 ml/kg/min. Additional submaximal treadmill data demonstrate that both Shorter and Clayton are metabolically economical runners and are able to use a larger fraction of their aerobic capacities (>85% $\dot{V}o_2$ max) during competition than most marathon runners (approx. 75-80% $\dot{V}o_2$ max).

What we learn from this research is that improving maximum oxygen consumption should not be the motivating factor in determining what training program we pursue as triathletes. In a sport that requires less than maximum effort over long distances, increasing our anaerobic threshold and/or increasing movement efficiency should be the criterion.

The four training programs which will improve aerobic performance are long slow distance training, short rest interval training, speed play, and pace training. When establishing a base level of training, long slow distance probably offers the highest yield with the least amount of risk to injury. Distances should increase gradually, not extending your distances by more than 10% of what your body has adapted to.

Once your base is established, other training programs should replace this below-pace training technique. The next logical step would be to train at or above your anaerobic threshold which will extend your maximum aerobic power and your ability to deal properly with high-lactic acid levels. The most effective training technique for this purpose is short rest interval training and should be done in all three events. Speed play, when done aggressively, will serve the same purpose, and allow you to mix up your anaerobic threshold training efforts. Injury risk is higher when speed is increased, so carefully monitor anaerobic threshold training with small and careful progressions.

Because triathlon performance demands optimal efficiency over strategic concerns such as drafting, breaking away, and outkicking the competitors at the finish, I feel that pace training should serve as the bulk of your workouts. The more you expose your body to the exact race demands in each event, the more efficient you will become.

Frequency of Training

The question of how often you should train in each event is subject to much debate. Most of the printed material on triathlon training leaves the reader with the impression that three workouts a day, every day is the accepted triathlon training technique. Not only am I skeptical whether anyone really does swim, bike, and run 7 days a week, but more importantly, I highly criticize the wisdom of such a program. After all, what makes for interesting reading is not the careful, logical training regimen, but the grueling astronomical miles through relentless terrain while being confronted with sharks, man-o-wars, fierce dogs, and killer bees.

In looking at the literature, it becomes apparent that you must train at least three times per week in order to realize improvement (Brynteson & Sinning, 1973). This, along with the specificity of training concepts previously introduced, suggest that the frequency data would apply to each individual sport. For the triathlete who needs training in three sports, this then means your total workout inventory is a minimum of nine workouts weekly, three in each sport.

At the other end of the spectrum, the general consensus among sport researchers is that working out six and seven times a week offers very little improvement in sport performance over the results experienced by exercising three or four times per week. Working out 6 and 7 days per week for the triathlete extrapolates out to suggest 18 and 21 weekly workouts, respectively. The minimal improvement yield of these higher workout rates, coupled with the greater risk of injury and illness, leave me apprehensive about recommending daily workouts in all three events. Based on these observations at the extreme ends of the frequency spectrum, the prudent rate of training then falls into the area of 3, 4 and 5 days training per week, or 9, 12, and 15 workouts per week as a triathlete. Determining how often you should train, leads us back to a group of traits that makes up one's final performance suggested in Table 4.1. Highly trained swimmers, for instance, who literally knife through the water, may not need the water hours that those with "brick bellies" do. Goals, strengths, weaknesses, and many other differences exist among individuals. Therefore, train at the frequency appropriate for your particular situation, not someone else's.

Training Principles Combined

Based on the training principles just described, we must now consider how they work in conjunction with each other. In review, triathletes need to train at least three times per week in each event but no more than five times weekly. Total number of workouts in a week will then be between 9 and 15. If you accept the pace-training concept, then the speed of your workouts will closely approximate speeds you intend to maintain in competition. Finally, the distances covered will progress gradually until you are close to the distances demanded of you in the race. Train as much as you can in conditions similar to those you would expect to find in your race. If your race is known for its heat, humidity, and hills, then you should try to train in the same environment.

Trying to squeeze in a minimum of nine workouts in 1 week means that you will have to do double workouts at least 2 days in the week. If you are working out 15 times in a week, you must perform double workouts every day, with a triple workout on one of those days. Some rationale should be behind the way you plan the sequence of your workouts. Consider the possible combinations of double workouts. You can swim and bike, bike and run, and swim and run. Based on the sequence required of you in competiton, train in the first two combinations with as little rest in between as possible. I call this transition training, and the order is very important.

In my first year of triathlon competition, I was a fairly inexperienced cyclist, training in the early mornings with a local cycle-racing club. After finishing the cycling, I would push hard all the way home, quickly change into my running clothes, and head out for a run. Not only did I complete my total day's training before my kids wiped the sand out of their eyes, but I also was training the physiological adjustments required by the bike/run transition.

The swim/bike training can be done in a similar fashion, if you can safely store your bike nearby your water environment. This sequence, however, is of little physiological concern because going from armwork to legwork can be performed with a few complications. Whenever I was confronted with a swim/run day, I would seldom, if ever, train the two in succession simply because the race does not demand it.

Overtraining

Overtraining is a common problem among the highly motivated, "driven" competitor but can occur even among those in the "middle-of-the-pack." By definition, overtraining is a condition in which an athlete's adaptive mechanisms are stressed to the point of failure. When the adaptive mechanisms fail, further training of a similar nature causes athletes to lose conditioning rather than to gain it.

In his book *Triathlon Training Manual*, Sisson (1983) vividly describes his frequent brushes with overtraining. If you are interested in studying this problem in great detail, I recommend reading his testimony on the problem.

The problem of overtraining stems from the locker room theory which suggests that if a little is good, more is better, and more than the competition is best. Although these people have very good intentions, they are overlooking the important need for rest and recovery. Would you expect your automobile to continually roll up the miles without some level of maintenance? Of course not. But because the body is capable of making most of its own repairs, we view it differently.

How then does the body tell us when it is falling behind in its ability to recover and maintain an adequate state of repair? This question can be answered by looking at the symptoms normally associated with overtraining.

A combination of physical and psychological problems stem from overtraining. Table 4.3 lists some of the symptoms that are associated with overtraining. Although these symptoms could indicate other conditions, they, nevertheless, are reliable indicators of overtraining, and in extreme cases of overtraining, most if not all of the symptoms are usually experienced.

Once you realize you're a victim of this performance-limiting problem, the question, then, becomes one of how to diagnose the origin of the problem, so it can be dealt with. Selye (1956) states that excessive stress is the cause of overtraining. The stressors are most often from both psychological and physiological

TABLE 4.3   Symptoms of Overtraining

General	Physical	Psychological
Poor practices	Loss of weight	Depression
Poor performances	Joint and muscle	Irritability
	Pain without injury	Insomnia
	Nausea	Anxiety
	Head colds, stuffy nose	

Note: From *Swimming Faster* (p. 374) by Ernest Maglischo, by permission of Mayfield Publishing Company. Copyright 1982 by Mayfield Publishing Company.

sources. Boredom, anxiety, fear, and loss of self-esteem are among the psychological stressors that may produce an overtrained state; the physiological stressors include excessive physical exercise, lack of sleep, poor nutrition, illness, and injury.

Maglischo (1982) cautions his readers that many athletes can become overtrained because they try too hard and care too much, rather than because they are lazy and lack motivation. If not diagnosed properly, athletes may tend to doubt their dedication, their ability to compete, or worse yet, their adequacy as human beings.

The stressor with which athletes should be most concerned is excessive physical exercise. According to Miller and Mason (1964), the intensity of the training rather than the total distance seems to be a bigger problem leading to overtraining. The authors suggest that when overtraining is suspected, 1 to 3 days of low-intensity anaerobic threshold training may offer the necessary relief. If this program fails, it may be necessary to allow 2 to 5 days of complete rest.

Preventing overtraining appears to be successful when variety is incorporated into your training program. This variety should include training at different intensities, modalities, and distances. Sisson and others recommend a combination of hard-easy-hard-easy workouts as a prudent preventive measure for overtraining. This concept may also be conducive toward injury prevention as well.

Chapter 5

Swim Training

Swimming brings to the triathlon the most complicated set of limitations. As kids, we all became relatively efficient at bicycling and running without coaching or sophisticated equipment. We also learned how to swim; but for most, swimming for efficiency and conditioning was not a concern. We learned to swim merely to survive in and around the water. Swim lessons were designed to teach survival techniques with some attention given to traditional swimming strokes. Having passed the basic swimming courses, we were left to confront the occasional visits to the waterfront during selected seasons of the year, and we swam to have fun. Only a select few received any coaching on swim training and technique.

To the triathlete, these limitations should not spell doom, but rather present a more realistic picture of what changes may be needed to achieve swimming proficiency. Good swimmers make good triathletes not because the sport is weighted heavily in favor of the swim, but because good swimmers bring efficiency into the triathlon, where efficiency is the most difficult to acquire. Most everyone can develop swim efficiency, but it requires careful study of technique, good coaching, breaking away from old habits, and plenty of practice.

Then, what does it take to become an efficient swimmer? In reply, let us once again refer back to our developing years. One of the most popular excuses given to athletes possessing refined sport skills is that they are natural athletes. The assumption here is that these select few bring into their sport a variety of endowed virtues which brings rapid success with minimal effort. Remember the school jock who excelled in several sports throughout the year? Give him a ball, any ball, explain the rules, and he will produce. These athletes are often children of athletes, further reinforcing this natural athlete rationale.

Sport psychologists and experts in motor development have trouble with the natural athlete phenomenon; also, researchers find little evidence supporting this view. Sport success, according to the experts, is heavily related to the amount of positive exposure one experiences in a sport. During the developing years, the natural athlete was most likely exposed to many positive experiences with sport which facilitated success as a youth and continued throughout his or her competing years.

The principle of positive exposure is that we are attracted to experiences that create feelings of satisfaction and gratification, and that we tend to avoid negative experiences and exposures. The problem with becoming efficient swimmers in our youth was that positive exposure was hard to achieve, because for most, swimming created sociological limitations: The swim clubs were for the elite. Another problem preventing swimming efficiency is that the little coaching we received as children is considered inefficient by current standards because stroke technique has changed so drastically. Finally, when all things are considered, swimming is just a not a very convenient sport.

This chapter will discuss the mechanics of the front crawl relating to the triathlete's needs. Several volumes have been written on the intricacies of the front crawl movement discussing fluid mechanics and how they apply to proper movements. For detailed reading on the subject, I recommend *Swimming Faster* by Maglischo (1982), who effectively presents interpretable material to the lay reader. This chapter, however, will focus only on the front crawl because it is generally accepted as the most efficient stroke for the distances required in typical triathlons. The basic objectives of swim mechanics are (a) to maximize the propulsive force generated by your limbs, and (b) to minimize the resistance or drag that occurs as your body passes through the water.

Maximizing Propulsive Force

Most likely, we were taught to picture our hands moving through the water just like a paddle is used in canoeing. The more perpendicular our hands were to the force of direction, the more resistance and, therefore, the more forward motion we would produce. Not so, say the stroke mechanic experts such as Councilman (1977), Firby (1975), and Maglischo (1982). Granted, the paddle concept will teach the purpose adequately, but there is a more efficient way. Conceptualize the hand more as an airplane wing rather than a paddle. By pitching your hand with fingers together, the same mechanical principles of drag and lift that allow birds and planes to fly can provide more propulsive force from the hands when swimming the front crawl. Maglischo (1982) suggests using the concept of moving the hands like propeller blades rather than like paddles. In reality, the movement combines the two concepts (propellers and paddles) to create an ''S'' shape movement of the hand as it travels through the water. Figure 5.1 illustrates this movement.

The Armstroke

The armstroke in the front crawl is broken down into six phases: entry, catch, downsweep, insweep, upsweep, and recovery.

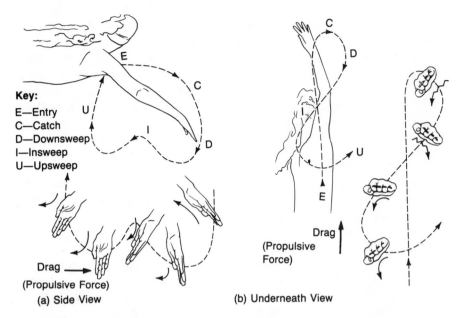

Key:
E—Entry
C—Catch
D—Downsweep
I—Insweep
U—Upsweep

Drag →
(Propulsive Force)
(a) Side View

Drag ↑
(Propulsive
Force)
(b) Underneath View

Figure 5.1 Arm patterns of the front crawl from (a) the side view and (b) the bottom view. Adapted from *Swimming Faster* by Ernest Maglischo. Copyright 1982 by Mayfield Publishing Company. Reprinted by permission.

Entry Phase. Entry is the point at which your hand and arm enter the water. This point should be forward of the head and about 8 to 10 inches short of full extension. Entry is slightly to the side of the body's midline with the palm facing outward 30 to 40 degrees. The thumb side of the hand should enter the water first. Once your hand enters the water, you should attempt to move the wrist, elbow, and shoulder through the same hole that was cut by your hand in the water.

Avoid overreaching and underreaching. Overreaching occurs when the entry is extended out so far that the hands cross the body's midline creating left/right movement in the trunk. Underreaching occurs when the entry is so short that the elbow does most of its extension underwater. Underreaching fails to maximize the stroke's potential and opposes forward motion.

Once your arm has entered the water, it should be extended in a smooth manner. Thrusting forward at this point resists forward motion, plus, it precedes the completion of the stroke from the opposite arm, putting you into an asynchronous state.

Catch Phase. As your arm extends and as your opposite arm is finishing its upsweep, flex the forward wrist downward approximately 40 degrees and rotate outward. At this point you should be able to feel a solid handful of water. Fingers are together (or only slightly apart), not allowing water to slip through.

Downsweep Phase. Here your hand should sweep downward and outward in a curvilinear path. This downward direction engages the "propeller" motion, and the backward movement simulates the "paddle" movement. Notice that the palm of the hand follows the path at a perpendicular angle to the body's midline. At the point where the downsweep is at its deepest, the hand then starts to rise, representing the beginning of the insweep. The purpose of the downsweep is not to generate great amounts of propulsion, but merely to get the arms in position for the two latter phases where greatest propulsion is generated. Cautiously avoid dropping the elbow during the downsweep. The elbow is above the wrist and moves naturally as long as the hand is being directed downward.

Insweep Phase. The insweep begins at the deepest point of the downsweep. The hand begins an inward and backward path. The insweep starts lateral to the midline of the body but finishes near or across the midline. Notice that the hand changes pitch as it moves through the center portion of the "S" sweep. As the hand begins its travel toward the midline of the body, the elbow flexes to allow the hand to rise upward, closer to the body.

The greatest difficulty in executing a proper insweep appears to be the pitch of the hand as it moves inward, upward, and backward. When you fail to change the pitch as the directions change, your hand tends to "slip" through the water without creating any propulsive force.

Upsweep Phase. The upsweep phase is a push backward from the chest to the waist, and then upward, outward, and backward until the elbow approaches full extension. Coaches suggest that if done properly, you should feel your thumb brush the outside of your thigh. When your hand approaches your thigh, the propulsive force is complete. Your hand should then rotate inward to release the pressure on the water and edge out with minimal drag. The upsweep is the most propulsive phase of the stroke, but many misinterpret its importance by pulling the hand out of the water at the waist, short of the midthigh.

Recovery Phase. Although the arm recovery does not contribute to the propulsion force, if poorly executed, it can result in compromised efficiency, timing, and body alignment. The objective of the recovery phase is to reposition the arm for another stroke. The preferred technique is with the high-elbow recovery because it is more efficient and does not disturb body alignment.

Recovery begins during the final stages of the upsweep. Here, the elbow breaks through the water while the hand is completing the upsweep. The elbow moves forward and upward while slightly flexed. As the shoulder rotates, the bend in the elbow becomes greater, causing the hand to follow close to the water's surface. The hand continues to move forward until it is repositioned to once again begin the entry phase of the stroke. Remember that the recovery is not a forced effort, but rather one that is smooth and relaxed. Tense muscles during the recovery phase will restrict valuable blood flow and ultimately lead to premature fatigue.

If the timing between the arms is correct, an arm will always provide propulsive force: While one arm completes the entry and begins the catch, the other arm is finishing the upsweep.

The Flutter Kick

I doubt swimmers spend many hours in heated argument over the role of the front crawl flutter kick, but some controversy appears concerning at least one of the roles the flutter kick serves. No one disputes its effectiveness in stabilizing the armstroke. In this capacity, the flutter kick balances out the otherwise exaggerated movements of the arms and also aids the body in maintaining a horizontal position.

Controversy does exist concerning how much the flutter kick contributes to forward propulsion. When you immobilize the arms by holding onto a kickboard, thus relying on the flutter kick for all forward motion, you quickly arrive at two observations: First, your forward motion is quite minimal when compared to the contribution made by the arms and second, you quickly realize how fatiguing this experience is. Researchers have observed that the flutter kick requires four times the energy output to cover the same distance as using arms only. Thus, distance swimmers and those others needing to conserve their energy supply should perform the flutter kick only enough to stabilize, sacrificing its propulsive role in favor of efficiency.

The flutter kick can best be broken down into two distinct movements: the downbeat and the upbeat. Picture the lower leg as if it were loosely attached; the thigh tends to lead the lower leg throughout its entire movement (see Figure 5.2). The lower leg continues to sweep downward with the knee flexed 30 to 40 degrees and the toes pointed as much as possible. At the end of the downbeat, the foot should be 12 to 14 inches deep but only slightly deeper than your chest.

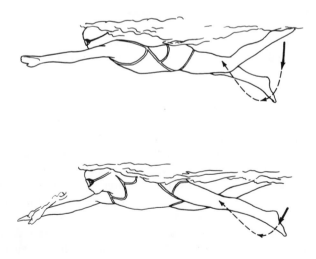

Figure 5.2 Leg patterns of the flutter kick. Adapted from *Swimming Faster* by Ernest Maglischo. Copyright 1982 by Mayfield Publishing Company. Reprinted by permission.

In the upbeat portion of the kick, the hip and knee once again lead to the movement, so that even before the foot completes the downward segment, the hip and knee are beginning the upbeat phase. The feet are still pointed from the ankle but not forcefully so.

In coordinating the arm and leg movements into proper timing, first determine the number of kicks per stroke cycle. Variations appear to consist of either two, four, or six beats per complete stroke cycle (two armstrokes). When the need to conserve energy is critical, the two-stroke kick is the apparent choice; however, when optimal speed is the issue, then the four- and six-beat kicks have relevance.

In the two-beat kick there are two kicks per arm cycle, or one down and upbeat per armstroke. Arm turnover is generally faster using a two-beat kick. If you find yourself "sinking" when using a two-beat kick, then you will need to incorporate a four- or six-beat kick.

Minimizing Resistance or Drag

Efficient swimmers appear to "knife" through the water with little effort: They execute proper stroke mechanics effectively, and their cardiovascular efficiency is, no doubt, well adapted to the task. These human torpedoes have also refined one other area of their stroke—minimal body drag.

Horizontal and Lateral Alignment

The overall objective in minimizing body drag is to streamline yourself as much as possible in the direction you are moving. Horizontal and lateral alignment are the topics of concern here. In horizontal alignment (best viewed from the side) make every effort to keep your body as parallel to the surface of the water as possible. The water line should be approximately at your hairline with your eyes focused forward and downward. Even when you roll to one side to take a breath, still maintain this linear position. Poor horizontal alignment can occur from kicking too deeply. Remember, you should kick only slightly lower than an imaginary line extending backward from the deepest part of your trunk.

Lateral alignment is best viewed from the top as it represents the degree to which the hips and legs stay in line (left and right) with the trunk. Poor lateral alignment occurs when the hips and legs swing outward from behind the trunk and is generally caused from overreaching at the entry portion of the armstroke. The result is a movement with an "S" shaped pattern incorporated in the forward motion. Pulling the head backward while breathing also causes poor lateral alignment.

When cutting through the water, the lateral and horizontal alignments work together to make the smallest hole possible. When arms and legs work well together with proper alignment, a definite "roll" from side to side occurs naturally. This roll not only allows the arms to rise effectively out of the water in the return and entry phases, but is also important for effective breathing. Rotating at least 45 degrees to each side from the horizontal, this side-to-side roll is seldom overexaggerated.

Breathing

Coordinating all the above movements into one fluid motion is difficult enough without adding the important function of breathing. (I hope all fish realize how good they have it.)

Turning your head sideward to breathe should be incorporated into the body roll. When you are rolled maximally toward your breathing side, your mouth should be exposed to the air temporarily without any exaggeration of body roll and with only minimal extra roll of the head. Begin turning your head when the arm opposite the breathing side enters the water. This allows your head roll to precede the body roll and add extra time to expose your mouth above water for that all important breath.

Returning your face to the water should also be coordinated with your body roll. Practice exhaling while your face is underwater, but don't exhale completely. If you should find a wave instead of air at your mouth's next opening, you'll be glad some of that last breath was saved. Maintaining a small air reserve also aids in buoyancy.

Swim Training Program

Prior to developing a swim training program, you must establish a target distance to proficiency, and then set a target date for accomplishing your objective. This can be a problem for triathletes because of the varying swim distances that triathlons require. Triathlon swim distances vary from ½ mile to 2.4 miles; this plays havoc on training if you're a frequent competitor.

Let me reinforce once again the tremendous need for coaching when you are developing stroke technique. The separation of mind and body experienced as you enter the water prohibits the opportunity to self-critique. Seeing correct form in books, in other swimmers, and even in yourself on videotape will certainly help, but you still need another set of trained eyes to follow the development of your stroke. Your coach should review your stroke mechanics regularly and contribute ideas for improvement.

Correction should be in small enough doses so you can incorporate change without confusion. Remember, *practice makes permanent, not perfect*—so don't train with blatant errors in your stroke mechanics. My initial training in the water was done with fingers widely spread apart in the catch phase. I had actually perfected this method before my coach pointed out the gross error in efficiency. Correcting the mistake set my training schedule back almost a whole month!

Depending on your skill level, begin swim training early enough in your training to allow time for mastering stroke mechanics. Pool swimming serves this purpose quite well.

The next level of training should be to lay down your distance training base. Once again, this should consist of long continuous swimming at moderate intensity. An ideal setting for this type of training would be in open water although a swimming pool can be used. When base training, concentrate on proper stroke mechanics, especially when you feel fatigue encroaching upon you. Signs of a fatigued stroke include a shortened entry, a shortened upsweep, and a slower stroke cadence. *Don't continue training with improper stroke mechanics.* Better that you either conclude your workout, rest long enough to allow for the return of proper stroke mechanics, or incorporate a shorter duration interval workout.

At the conclusion of distance base training, you should be able to swim your target distance nonstop, maintain proper stroke mechanics throughout, and be free of soreness and injury, especially in the shoulder area. Assuming you meet these criteria, move into your more intense training program.

Without question, training for distance swimming requires sessions of long durations at a fairly intense pace. If you have a target pace established, then pace training should be a major part of your training program. You will further develop your aerobic capacity, but more importantly, you will familiarize your body to the demands required of you in competition.

As stated earlier, Maglischo (1982) cautions swimmers to avoid burnout while pace training, but his orientation is toward an all-out swim pace. Triathlon swimming is intense but still at less than maximal demands. Maglischo's concern for burnout does, nevertheless, apply to triathletes who need the variety in training to keep their enthusiasm high.

A good way to add variety while adding to the training effect would be to incorporate some short rest interval training into your program. If you have access to a pool, practice this technique by performing intervals on a send-off basis. A good example to illustrate this workout might be doing 10 X 100 yard intervals on 2 minute send-offs. Here you swim a hard 100 and rest for the remainder of the 2 minutes. With this technique, you never fully recover, and your anaerobic threshold and maximal oxygen consumption capacities are challenged. As you get in better shape, lower your send-off times and increase the interval distance and/or number of send-offs.

Swimming Particulars for the Triathlete

The oxygen needs for swimming is directly related to swimming efficiency. Poor swimmers are confronted with a kind of double jeopardy because their greater oxygen demands create a hurried or short-reaching stroke. Also, the sensation of always needing deep breaths of air can create tremendous anxiety in the triathlete.

For many triathletes, swimming is a necessary evil that must be tolerated. Triathletes who are poor swimmers must force themselves to spend time in the open water for many environmental reasons. The pool, with all the buoys, lifeguards, and nearby decks is a fine place to practice stroke mechanics; because you know that help is near, fear is minimized. Then when you find yourself practicing in open water without all those floating securities, anxiety tends to gnaw on your self-confidence, the confidence you gained back at the swim club.

Begin open water training when the water is relatively calm and warm enough to minimize the fears of hypothermia. Also helpful is to seek out a stretch of water shallow enough to stand up in should panic strike; have a friend escort your workout in a rowboat or surfboard—a good substitute if finding shallow water is a problem.

The initial experiences with open-water swimming will orient you to the motionless sensation experienced when you can no longer see the bottom passing beneath you. For some, this can be a frightening experience. I had a friend who was an excellent biker and runner but had never trained in the open water. In his first triathlon, although the swim phase was only a half mile out and back, he opted for a rowboat ride to shore with half the swim to go. He could not sense himself moving through the water and was unable to grasp the fact that if he were performing his stroke as usual, then he must be progressing through the water.

Swim training in the pool can also leave you with a false sense of confidence of your ability to swim straight. Just because you are not colliding with the lane buoys during your pool workout doesn't mean you will swim straight in open water. In fact, it's conceivable to swim in complete circles in open water if you were never to sight for direction. Even the most skilled swimmers can find themselves off-course because of currents and waves. All open-water swimmers respect the need to sight for direction.

In your early experiences with open-water swimming, you might practice sighting-off your floating escort, but sooner or later you must confront the problem of sighting. If you can clearly see landmarks while in the water, you can accomplish sighting by "peeking." The technique is as follows: Just before you normally return your face to the water after an inhalation, you turn your head forward, quickly locate your point of reference, and then submerge your face. Once back into your normal stroke, correct your direction by pulling wider with the arm opposite the direction you intend to go. This will reorient your lateral alignment without requiring you to stop, to shift, and to begin forward motion all over again.

In order to get your bearings if water is particularly rough or reference points small, you may have to incorporate a water polo stroke, which is the front crawl with the head out of the water for the entire stroke cycle. This movement requires an accentuated kick, so initial experiences with this technique can be exhausting. Practice this technique thoroughly before competing in open water. Most open-water swimmers will sight every five-to-eight stroke cycles.

Bilateral Breathing

Distance swimmers will often recommend using a bilateral breathing technique (breathing on both sides), which they claim helps to "round out" your stroke. The technique is a system whereby you breathe once every cycle and a half, instead of every cycle. Bilateral breathing teaches you to roll your body equally to both sides, causing you to develop equal pulling strength in both arms. Because of this balancing benefit, you will be able to swim in a straighter line.

Although these benefits are attractive, the quantity of oxygen made available to the lungs is compromised. Bilateral breathers come up with one less breath every three-stroke cycle when compared to those who practice the conventional breathing technique. This decrease in oxygen availability can result in premature fatigue, not to mention the anxiety associated with being in an oxygen deficit.

Those of you who need to balance out your stroke or who are attracted to the bilateral breathing technique for other reasons must practice at great lengths in order to increase breathing efficiency, thereby reducing the oxygen deficit problem.

Drafting

Another technique to improve your swimming in competition is to draft-off another swimmer. The technique is perfectly legal and can decrease your work output by as much as 30%! Employ the same theories that bikers use to draft, namely, to stay close to and in the same path of the swimmer ahead of you.

Finally, learn to accept distractions while swimming. Many swimmers train in water that is calm, clear, peaceful, and free of obstruction. Come race day, bodies are constantly encroaching your domain with others' arms and even feet getting tangled up in your stroke. Realize, however, that the competitors find no strategy in attempting to complicate your stroke. Like you, they are merely trying to survive and negotiate the same confrontations.

Equipment and Performance Aids

Fortunately, the complexity of the swimming technique is not met with expensive equipment, provided water is available. A snug-fitting nylon suit and goggles complete the equipment needs for competition. Because goggles leak, fog up, and get knocked ajar in competition, use caution when buying them; try on several pair and select the pair that best fits the contours of your face. For those of you with poor eyesight, consider purchasing prescription goggles. Even goggles that promote antifog virtues seldom stay fog-free when regularly used. To avoid foggy lenses, lick the inside of the lenses and then rinse them before putting on the goggles. Another technique is to leave a little water or saliva in each goggle before putting them on. If they fog up, put your head straight down and move your head about until the water clears the lens. If your goggles begin to leak in competition, don't panic: Turn onto your back, pull the goggles away from your face, make the necessary adjustments, and resume your normal stroke.

Again, practice this technique, so you can perform it when it's needed—and needed fast.

Training aids are often used to isolate either the legs or arms. This allows the swimmer to practice the technique on one set of limbs only. When working with arm-stroke mechanics, swimmers often use pull buoys, a pair of styrofoam cylinders attached together with rope. These devices are placed between the thighs and are locked in place when the legs squeeze together. Kick boards can also be used, but they tend to limit the natural body rotation.

To help you get a proper feel for the water, use paddles. These devices strap around the wrist and middle finger creating a full and flat surface on the palm of the hand. If your hand pitches diagonally to the water instead of perpendicularly, you will feel a slipping motion. Paddles are also used to strengthen shoulder muscles because they increase the pulling surface area. Kick boards are best used when practicing leg-stroke mechanics. With head up, you hold onto a styrofoam board and commit all physical and mental energies to the kick.

Chapter 6

Man and His Machine

When considering all means of travel powered by physical effort, the bicycle emerges as the quickest and most efficient. Even the human-powered flight across the English Channel could have been performed more quickly given the same distance by road using a bicycle (Allen, 1979). Cyclists with special equipment, refined skill, and stamina have frequently been clocked at speeds in excess of 100 mph while drafting behind motorized vehicles.

Whether it was the speed, efficiency, or simply happenstance that brought the bicycle into the triathlon, it is the most contrasting type of physical performance that can be compared to swimming. Where swimming falls short on speed and equipment, cycling incorporates both to a great degree. Where cycling is short on biomechanics, swimming requires a refined technique. Finally, where swimming is sociologically limiting, cycling is accepted and used by everyone at all ages.

This chapter will describe what I consider to be the ideal triathlon "machine," how to fit your body to this machine, and then will deal with cycling mechanics. I will also investigate training techniques specifically for triathlon competition and conclude with a discussion on bicycle maintenance.

The Machine

Upon entering a bicycle shop, you, no doubt, are overwhelmed by all the different brands and types of bicycles displayed before you. Except for size, all appear similar. When deciding what type is best for your triathlon needs, first consider the two different types of frames.

Based on function, bicycle frames are either of a touring design or a racing design or a hybrid of the two, popularly called a "sport" frame. Touring frames are designed to provide the cyclist with a more comfortable ride. In order to accomplish this, the front forks are curved more at the ends, allowing more road shock to be absorbed before the vibrations are felt in the hands. The head tube angle (forward pitch of the fork) is less than in racing frames, again minimizing road vibration. Finally, the gearing on a touring frame is designed for a slow, steady ride carrying heavy loads on roads requiring steep ascents.

In contrast, the racing frame is designed to transfer all energies into a forward direction. To do so, the fork is much straighter and the head tube angle more vertical. Because of this design, shock absorbency and riding comfort are sacrificed, but the added stiffness allows more effort to be transferred to the wheels instead of being absorbed by the flexible frame. Also, the steeper angles create a difference in handling, making the racing frame less stable and more responsive. It is interesting to note, however, that stability is appreciably improved when speeds approach 20 mph.

Between the touring and the racing frame designs emerges the sport frame design. Here, we have a bit of controversy as to the effectiveness of this frame in serving both touring and racing needs. Some feel the sport frame is for the "overnight cycling" tourist who needs frame strength to carry small loads, but not the comfort required in cycling successive 100+ mile days. Racing enthusiasts are attracted to its medium weight and lower cost but still view this frame as a compromise in speed and responsiveness.

What we need in a triathlon frame is a design that will not require a compromise in performance, yet will not leave the triathlete so stiff and sore that he must be "unglued" from the bike. Performance and comfort—is it possible to have both?

The Triathlon Frame

If you modify the full-on racing frame by adding a few "touring" type characteristics, you can achieve both performance and comfort. First, begin by shortening the handle bar stem. In racing bicycles, this stem is quite long allowing the racer to stretch out on his frame. Racing in this position is more aerodynamic, and it also places the hip extensor muscles in a better position to apply pedal force. This racing position is fine for a 25-mile time trial but will leave the triathlete in a sad state for the run that follows. A shorter stem will reduce such a stretched-out position.

Next, replace the inflexible racing saddle with a padded touring saddle. The Avocet touring saddle series works well, but much more comfortable racing saddles are available. The Concourse and Turbo saddles have become welcomed additions to many racing frames. These saddles have the typical racing saddle features of being narrow and lightweight but are still supple and comfortable.

Padding the handlebars is the next step. The Spenco grips are most impressive. Added padding offered by riding gloves can increase riding comfort to all types of grips. Get riding gloves for this reason as well as for cleaning your tires of road glass and gravel while you are in motion. (More on this later.)

Outfitting the Frame

Let us now consider the components to complete your frame. Some of the terminology can get rather technical, so use Figure 6.1 to aid you in identifying the components being discussed.

The wheels and tires are the components which together can most affect the bike's riding characteristics, cornering ability, load-carrying tasks, acceleration, and for the triathlete—efficiency as reflected in minimal rolling resistance. Hubs are either large flange or small flange, depending on need. Large flange hubs supposedly give a stiffer ride which allows more pedal torque to be forwarded through the shorter spokes and into the tires. However, the trade-off is stiffness. Small flange hubs serve a softer ride because there is more spoke length to absorb road shock. Because the difference is nearly undetectable, I suggest you merely take what your dealer has in stock. Triathletes are now finding good success in hubs with fewer spokes than with the standard 36-spoke hubs. With a 32-spoke hub, for instance, the fewer spokes create less wind resistance and are lighter. Those who weigh in at 170 lbs or more should be advised against the idea, as fewer spokes create a more fragile rim.

One final problem confronting you in deciding on hubs is whether or not to get sealed bearing hubs. These hubs are designed to require less maintenance, which may also allow you to use the hubs longer before replacing them. The trade-off for the virtue of low maintenance is rolling resistance. There is a definite compromise in rolling resistance between the sealed and the standard bearing hubs. Turn the spindles of the two different types for comparison and then judge for yourself. If you find yourself frequently training in rain or on dusty, windy roads, consider using sealed bearings. Otherwise, stick with standard bearing hubs and enjoy maximum efficiency.

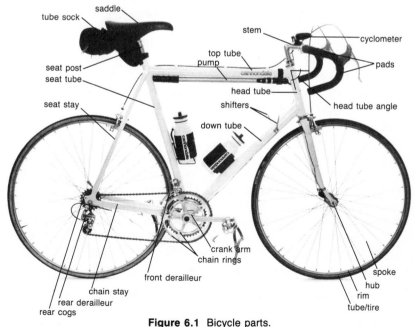

Figure 6.1 Bicycle parts.

Your choice of spokes is between the butted or the straight gauge types. Butted spokes are thinner throughout the length of the spoke, except for reinforcement in the last 2 in. of both ends where strength is most important. Straight gauge spokes are of the same diameter throughout. If you are fairly light, you may benefit by saving on wind resistance and weight if you use butted spokes. If you are heavier or capable of applying great amounts of torque or find yourself on rough roads, then be safe and go for the strength benefit of straight gauge spokes. Rim selection can be very difficult if you don't have a specific purpose in mind. But before deciding on a rim, you must make a major decision as to which of the two types of tube and tire systems to use: the clinchers or the tubulars. With clinchers, the tire is separate from the tube. This is the most conventional design where the tires are held to the rims by mating the wire circumference of the tire over the metal bead on the rim. The tube consumes space in the tire and rim, and when inflated, keeps the wire from popping off the rim (see Figure 6.2).

Until recently, clinchers were associated with "throw-away" quality bikes. These tires were big and heavy, carried low-inflation ratings, and were simply lacking in performance. Because the clincher system carried with it some excellent virtues, designers began creating smaller, lighter, and higher pressure capabilities to the point where manufacturers are now considering clincher tire performance as comparable to tubular tires.

Tubular tires are a completely different system in that the tube and tire are inseparable. The tire casing completely encompasses the tube, and the casing walls are then sewn together. For this reason, tubular tires are often called "sew-ups." The tubular rim in cross section is concave to receive the convex curvature of the tire. Proper mating of tire to rim is finalized when special glue is applied to prevent the tire from shifting or rolling off in fast, tight turns. Figure 6.2 illustrates the design differences between the two tire systems.

These design differences enable us to compare the advantages and disadvantages of the two systems. Table 6.1 categorizes these comparisons.

Doughty (1983) in his book *The Complete Book of Long Distance and Competitive Cycling* presents a racer's opinion of the two tire systems in discussion.

> The advantages of riding on tubular tires are real enough that many serious cyclists are willing to put up with the extra expense and maintenance. For a long time we had no choice because no clincher could come close to matching a tubular's performance. With its tube completely enclosed, a tubular can be inflated as high as 140 psi (some racing models), and this, plus its narrowness and lightness, provides markedly reduced rolling resistance. Rims for tubulars are always a light alloy for increased efficiency and responsiveness with different weights available to meet a rider's needs. But tubular rims, like the tires themselves, are more expensive than their clincher counterparts. They also tend to be less durable, though this can be overcome to a great extent if rim weight is correctly matched to riding conditions.
>
> The weight and performance characteristics of clinchers are in line with the average tubular. My only note of caution is that the new clinchers don't yet appear to have the rubber compounds and tread designs to equal the road-holding ability of tubulars.

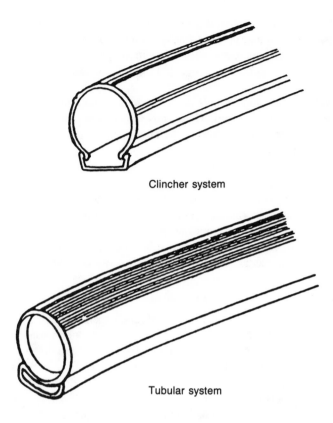

Clincher system

Tubular system

Figure 6.2 Tubular and clincher systems compared.

TABLE 6.1 **Advantages and Disadvantages of the Different Rim Systems.**

Tubulars	Clinchers
1. More expensive	1. Less expensive
2. Time consuming to patch	2. Easy to patch
3. Requires glueing	3. More prone to flats from spokes and tire irons
4. Less availability	4. Readily available
5. Fast and easy to change	5. Slightly heavier system
6. Overall a lighter system	6. Slightly more rolling resistance
7. Can take higher tire pressures	7. Slightly harder to change a flat
8. Superior handling and traction	8. Satisfactory handling and traction

Not only do you have to decide if you will go with a clincher type tire or a tubular type, but you must also contend with the rim width, strength, and weight. Please attempt to match your body weight to rim weight.

From here, you need to decide how important rolling resistance is to you. If you are seeking the path of least rolling resistance, you will opt for the tubular rims. If you find that the simple things in life are most important, then consider working with a narrow clincher rim. These rims should be no more than 25 mm wide because wider rims will not accept the now popular narrow profile tires that claim minimal rolling resistance.

Whatever rim and tire system you choose, make sure you run the tires at proper inflation ratings. Underinflated tires will increase rolling resistance by about 12% for every 20 lbs reduction in inflation pressure (Faria & Cavanagh, 1976). Not only is underinflating inefficient, but it is also dangerous. Low profile tires require optimal inflation in order to elevate the rim off the road's surface. Soft tires allow for the tire and tube to be pinched between the rim and a bump or road debris. When this occurs, a blowout, bent rim, or both can result.

Reliability

We have now dealt with the two most important (and expensive) considerations in developing your triathlon bike. What remains is purchasing components with proven reliability, for the components remaining have very little effect on performance and rolling resistance. Reliability must be realized from two perspectives: the ability to stand up to the many stresses that cyclists demand (durability), and the ability to perform year after year (wearability). Certainly, consider factors such as weight and responsiveness when building up the rest of your bike, but even "disposable" components can profess these virtues. Durability and wearability must be considered when purchasing the drive train, brakes, stem, and bars. Among the better component lines marketed for quality frames are Campagnolo, Shimano Dura-Ace, and Suntour Superbe. Shimano and Suntour also carry quality midpriced lines, such as the Shimano 600Ex and the Suntour Cyclone series.

Components of midprice quality or less will seldom carry replacement parts, which can be very frustrating, reflecting a compromise in quality. One other concern with your selection of components relates to the interchangeability between brands. Some of the Shimano drive train line, for instance, will not accept intervention by other brands.

Manufacturers have been active in creating frames and components with much attention given to aerodynamics. Frame tubes take on a tear drop shape, brake cables are threaded within the handlebar taping, and even the spokes on the wheels are tapered instead of round on both sides. Data from Gross, Kyle, and Malewicki (1983) suggest that at 20 mph the same rider assuming the same riding position on equally weighted bikes with the same tires and tire pressure will have to overcome 3.27 lbs of force to maintain a 20 mph speed on an aerodynamically equipped bike as compared to 3.48 lbs of force on a bike lacking aerodynamic modifications. This difference reflects approximately a 6% greater efficiency from using a bike aerodynamically equipped. Although this difference is worth noting, the real cycling economics come from the position you assume on the bike.

In summary, building your triathlon bike can be an enjoyable experience, but not one that newcomers to the bicycling field should attempt. Local bikers are always willing to talk at length about the details of tackling such an effort. Use their expertise if it is available. As you build your bike, you will better understand how to maintain, adjust, and repair it. The triathlon event requires that all repairs and adjustments be performed without support, so knowledge in these areas can pay off financially and performancewise as well.

Fitting Your Body to the Machine

Assuming you have avoided the expense of a frame custom built for your specific anatomy, the next step should be to "custom adjust" the bike to fit your body. As you purchase various components to build up your bike, you must be prepared to specify thread design, seat post diameter, and some components based on the various physical dimensions of your body.

Four bike parts require foreknowledge of body size when purchasing. They are, of course, the frame size, the stem length, the length of the crank arms, and the toe clips.

Frame Size

To determine the proper frame size, several techniques are commonly used. Store clerks usually have you straddle the top tube, and when there appears to be about a one inch clearance between your crotch and the top tube, the frame size is correct. This method, however, fails to consider differences in wheel and tire size and bottom bracket ground clearance, which could lead to a sizing error of as much as 2 inches. Frame size must be determined based on your leg length. De la Rosa and Kolin, in their book *The Ten-Speed Bicycle* (1979) suggest the following technique:

> Measure the distance from the head of the femur to the floor (in bare feet). Subtract 13.75 inches (34 centimeters) from that measurement to determine the correct frame size.

Figure 6.3 pictures the skeletal anatomy needed to perform this technique correctly. The head of the femur can be felt by turning the foot in and out (leg rotation).

Next, position the saddle for proper height, tilt, and position, front to back. When properly adjusted, the saddle's surface will be horizontal or tilted slightly up at the neck. Saddle height is a very important concern because it greatly influences your mechanical efficiency and injury potential. Hamley and Thomas

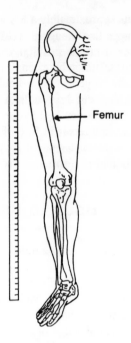

Figure 6.3 Measurement needed in determining correct frame size.

(1967) pointed out that every 4% change in saddle height can affect power output by approximately 5%. Saddle heights too high and too low can create havoc with the knees which will be discussed in chapter 11. Researchers Shennum and

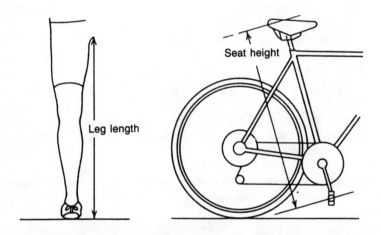

Figure 6.4 Setting proper seat height measurement. From *The Physiology and Biomechanics of Cycling* (p. 100) by I. Faria and P. Cavanagh, 1978, New York: John Wiley & Sons, Inc. Reprinted by permission.

deVries (1976) suggest a practical technique for approximating the ideal saddle height. While standing upright and wearing cycling shoes, feet 12 in. apart, measure from the floor to your crotch. Take this value and multiply by 1.09. This distance represents the distance from the axle of the pedal to the top of the seat as shown in Figure 6.4.

Realize that individual differences may require you to make some small adjustments from this setting. Whatever height you set your saddle, be careful your hips do not drop with each spin of the pedal. If your hips rock from side to side, the saddle height is probably set too high.

Most saddles are mounted on rails, allowing you to move the saddle forward and backward about 3 in. This adjustment is made while sitting on the saddle, both feet in the toe clips with the pedal crank arms horizontal to the ground. Position the saddle so that the center of the knee falls through the pedal's axle which is in the forward position. A string taped to the knee's center and weighted on

Figure 6.5 Horizontal adjustment of the saddle. Setting a ruler on the top of the saddle allows you to check for horizontal positioning. Stem height can also be checked during this measurement. With the ruler horizontal from the saddle, the stem height should be approximately 1 inch shorter.

Figure 6.6 Forward and backward adjustment of the saddle. Proper positioning places the groove behind the kneecap directly over the axle of the pedal, when the pedal is positioned at 3 o'clock.

the other end will help in making this measurement more exact. Figures 6.5 and 6.6 demonstrate the two techniques for proper saddle adjustment.

Toe Clips and Shoes

Next, comes the need to secure the foot properly into the pedals. Minimum equipment for this effort is toe clips, but this function is best performed when cleated cycling shoes are added. If you can't break loose for cycling shoes, then go on a transportation and hunger strike until you save the $30—I feel they are that important. Toe clips come in small, medium, and large based on shoe size. Cycling shoes must fit the foot snuggly yet be free enough to keep the foot from cramping. When the cleat is properly adjusted, the ball of the foot is directly over the pedal axle, and the inside heel of the foot clears the crank arm by about a quarter of an inch.

Fitting the Upper Body

All adjustments to this point have been concerned with fitting the lower body to the bike. The only opportunities of fitting the upper body are in selecting the correct handlebar stem length, the stem height, and the pitch of the handlebars. It would be most ideal if you could coerce your favorite bike dealer to determine proper stem length by using an adjustable stem. Stem adjustment can get very technical, as racers use this measurement to distribute body weight on each wheel, allowing for a more stretched-out position. The triathlete needs a stem length conservative enough to allow for a "comfortable" position: That is, not so short that you're left too upright (poor aerodynamics), but not so long that you're stretched out onto the bike. Make this adjustment with the hands located on the drops of the handle bar, wrists straight. Stem height should be about one inch lower than the top of the saddle (see Figure 6.5).

Stems are also designed to allow for adjustments in the handlebar pitch. Here, the flat portion of the handlebars, called the drops, should be pointing downhill. When properly adjusted, the wrists will come directly down onto the drops without having to bend.

Biomechanics of Cycling

Now that you are properly fitted and outfitted with your ideal triathlon bike, your efforts should now focus on cycling techniques. Resist the constant temptation to upgrade your bike in efforts to achieve that small percentage of gain on the competition. Knowledge of proper cycling mechanics, applied in a concentrated training strategy is the way cycling performance is achieved. Don't be surprised to find yourself pedaling alone in this effort. Few individuals are willing to invest the time and concentrated hard work needed to improve cycling skills. Unfortunately, it's all too easy to be a "bike techie": to know all the cycling jargon, to have all the right equipment, and to know all the big names in the sport. But when it actually comes time to perform, they're still working on a base training program.

In keeping with the principle that practice makes permanent, proper cycling mechanics must be permanently ingrained in your mind and ready to be applied to all workouts. Cyclists who lack this prerequisite understanding will eventually perfect their mistakes to the point where progress ceases or injury ensues.

Pedaling Efficiency

Developing pedaling efficiency is probably the cyclist's greatest concern; therefore, the techniques of pedaling mechanics and pedal cadence must be perfected properly. The basic principle in pedaling mechanics is to develop smooth circular strokes with fairly even pressure applied throughout a large part of the stroke circle. Most cyclists feel they pedal this way because the crank arms lead them through a circular pattern. But what generally happens is the applied force takes on more of an up/down piston-type stroke. When the muscles contract in circles, they cooperate with the crank arms to give a smooth, even pressure throughout. Think circles, not pistons. Pedal pressure applied in a piston-like manner utilizes primarily the powerful hip extensor muscle group called the gluteal muscles with most of the work coming from the gluteus maximus. The muscles that create knee flexion and extension also contribute little to this movement; the knee merely serves as a hinge allowing for the circular pedal motion to complete its course. Pedaling in smooth, even-pressured circles assists the work of the gluteal muscles by incorporating some knee extension and knee flexion during appropriate phases of the entire circular pedal motion. Whether one pedals in an up/down piston-like motion or in a circular motion, the maximum torque (rotational force) starts just forward of the top of the stroke and begins to lose its power just after the forward horizontal position, or from approximately 1 o'clock to 4 o'clock. The piston-type peddler works mainly in this area, using the hip extensor muscles almost exclusively and letting momentum move the pedals into proper position for the opposite hip to take action. If you find yourself shifting back and forth on your seat with each pedal rotation, you are probably pedaling in this fashion. Correct pedaling action begins sooner and involves extra muscle groups to round out the stroke.

Preceding the action of the hip extensors is the force applied by the knee extensor muscle group called the quadriceps, or "quads." As is shown in Figure 6.7a, the gluteals begin applying force to the knee in a forward horizontal direction at approximately 11 o'clock. Once the pedal is in the forward quadrant, the gluteal muscles contribute to the movement allowing for torque to be applied both in a forward and downward direction (see Figure 6.7b). After the crank arm reaches the forward horizontal position, the quads will no longer contribute to the movement since the pedal is ultimately forward at this point. In order to smooth out the stroke and increase efficiency, the quads need to gradually taper off the applied force and allow for a new muscle group to gradually exert power at the 4 o'clock position. A pull to the rear compliments the downward force still being applied by the hip extensors. This added torque is created by contracting the knee flexors, a muscle group located in the posterior thigh collectively called the hamstrings. Figure 6.7c shows that the hamstrings begin a pull on the crank arms to the rear from approximately 4 o'clock to 7 o'clock. During most of the phase where the hamstrings are working, the gluteals are resting because the downward torque tends to lose its effectiveness somewhere around 4 to 5 o'clock.

In effect, there are three distinct muscle groups involved in proper pedaling mechanics: The quads initiate the movement at the 11 o'clock position; the gluteals compliment the work at about the 1 o'clock position; the work of the quads is complete at about 3 o'clock; and the hamstrings take over and complete the stroke around the 7 or 8 o'clock position. As contraction of the hamstrings tapers off, the quads begin contracting. This technique is by far superior to the piston-like pedaling technique because added muscle mass is contributing torque on the crank arms. Muscles working collectively better distribute the work allowing for greater efficiency.

Figure 6.8 shows arrows of varying lengths being applied against the circle in different directions. The size of the arrow indicates the amount of force being

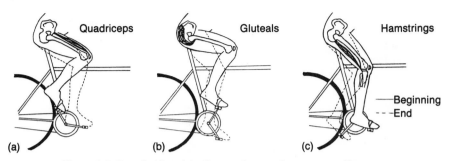

Figure 6.7 Coordination of the three major muscle groups used in proper pedaling mechanics.

applied, and the direction of the arrows shows the direction in which the force is applied. The authors (Faria & Cavanagh, 1976) make the following observations based on the arrow sizes and directions:

> Notice that the subjects were exerting very small forces as the pedal came over what we call top dead center (TDC), and the forces rose progressively throughout the first quadrant. The maximum value is usually reached at about 120 degrees—that is, 30 degrees past the horizontal. Next, notice how the arrow is pointing forward at the top of the power stroke and pointing back by the bottom of the stroke. Finally, note that there were still forces with a downward component during the recovery part of the cycle.
>
> It is very interesting to note what happens during the recovery phase. The force on the pedal never falls to zero, even though the subjects were wearing toe clips and cleated shoes. If the subjects had been actively pulling up on the pedal, the arrows would indicate upward forces but you see that they never do. Several experiments have confirmed that in relatively moderate riding situations, toe clips appear to be useful simply because they keep the foot in the correct position on the pedal. It is likely that in more taxing situations, such as hill climbing, the toe clips are used to exert upward forces, but the exact amount of benefit they give still remains to be determined.

The authors go on to say that the small downward arrows shown in the recovery phase of the stroke represent "lazy leg action." While one leg exerts maximum torque on the pedal, the opposite leg is carried around the circle until once again in position to apply force.

To avoid confusion, I must clarify or distinguish at this point the stroke mechanics of a sprint cyclist with those of an endurance-oriented cyclist. When a cyclist sprints, several additional muscle groups are utilized: muscles that move the ankle, plus more of the thigh muscles. Instead of beginning the pedal force at 11 o'clock and concluding at 8 o'clock, the rest phase between 8 and 11 o'clock is eliminated because the hamstrings contract throughout most of the circle. In addition, one of quadricep muscles (rectus femoris) is capable of hip flexion and, therefore, contracts between 7 o'clock and 12 o'clock to help pull up on the pedal until it is in position for all of the quads to begin extending the knee.

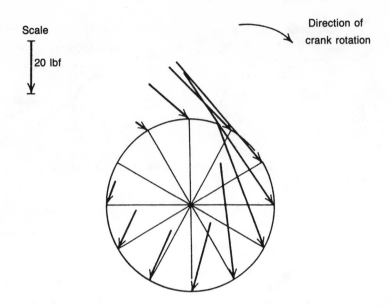

Figure 6.8 Direction and intensity of forces being applied to the pedals when proper pedal mechanics are in effect. From *The Physiology and Biomechanics of Cycling* (p. 91) by I. Faria and P. Cavanagh, 1978, New York: John Wiley & Sons, Inc. Reprinted by permission.

A technique called ankling is used lower down the leg which adds torque by forcing the toes downward in the forward phase of the stroke and by pulling the toes upward as the pedal returns to the top of the stroke (see Figure 6.9).

Recent studies (Smith & Gaston, 1984; Faria & Cavanagh, 1978) have shown the ankling movement to be more of a misnomer than what actually occurs in the stroke. For greatest efficiency, the pedal stroke should follow the natural motion of the foot. Efforts to exaggerate the foot motion create premature fatigue because it shortens the foot's rest phase. Because blood flows through a muscle only when it is not contracting, oxygen and other vital nutrients are limited, resulting in high levels of lactic acid and fatigue. This natural motion of the foot is compared to ankling in Figure 6.9.

The ultimate objective for sprinting is speed with little regard for efficiency. Considering the distances of a typical time trial or criterium race (approximately 25 miles), the trained cyclist can well afford to expend tremendous amounts of energy and generate high levels of lactic acid. But, for the triathlete, these techniques would only offer another excuse to wait for the sag wagon.

Triathletes need to be concerned with optimal performance in the context of efficiency. By pedaling in even-pressured circular movements, utilizing the hip extensors and both sets of thigh muscles, cyclists can be assured that their training will progress optimally.

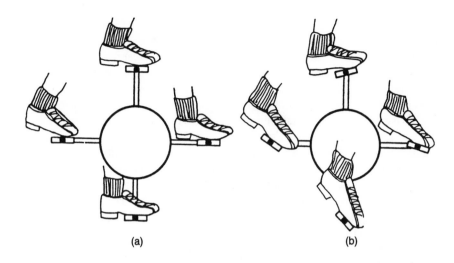

(a)   (b)

Figure 6.9 (a) Natural motion of the foot compared to (b) the ankling motion. From *The Physiology and Biomechanics of Cycling* (p. 104) by I. Faria and P. Cavanagh, 1978, New York: John Wiley & Sons, Inc. Reprinted by permission.

Once this pedaling movement is well developed, it must then be combined with proper pedal cadence. Pedal cadence refers to the number of revolutions (cycles) completed per minute. For the touring cyclist, pedal cadence is somewhere between 60 and 80 cycles per minute. Competitive cyclists seldom fall below a 90 cadence and can usually pedal effectively as high as 120. For the energy conscious triathlete, the range will probably fall between 70 to 90 cycles per minute and more realistically between 80 to 90.

As was mentioned earlier, blood flows through muscles only when they are in a relaxed state. But muscles in contraction can also aid in blood flow because blood is squeezed forward when the muscle is contracted. The trick, then, becomes an effort to create a contraction/relaxation rate which will allow optimal blood flow through the muscle. Slow pedal cadences will actually stop blood flow momentarily because the contractile phase is too long. High cadences, on the other hand, use so many additional muscle groups in an effort to stabilize the joints being radically thrashed around. Settle in on a cadence comfortable for you but attempt to maintain a rate somewhere between a 70 and 90. As you become more skilled and efficient, you will undoubtedly work longer at cadences closer to 90 than 70.

To check cadence, you will need either an electronic bicycle speedometer with a cadence display or a watch capable of displaying seconds. After you are thoroughly warmed up and are on a flat road, time the number of complete revolutions you pedal in a minute. This is not the most exact way, but a ready reference would be to make sure you are cycling at cadences faster than 1 per second and no faster than 3 revolutions every 2 seconds.

Gearing

Once you have settled in on an ideal cadence, you should try to maintain that rate throughout your entire workout with the possible exception of hills. To do so, you will need to carefully select proper gearing based on your abilities and the terrain you will be confronting. Proper gearing allows you to put forth approximately the same amount of effort at all times. Most low to moderately priced bikes have gearing that is totally unacceptable for this objective. Gearing on these bikes is set up with a massive spread between the smallest and the largest cogs on the freewheel. Wide ranges leave big gaps between gears; consequently, riders may find themselves spinning frantically in one gear and then muscling away in the next gear. A technique you may find effective is to have gears very close in the range where most of your riding is done, but have the last two gears in the rear cog spread out further to accommodate the hills. Since rear clusters are rather cheap and easy to change, carry several along and decide which gear range to use after reviewing the course. When I train in my local area, I use a rear cluster with a 13-14-15-17-19 arrangement on 52- and 42-tooth front chainrings. Since my area is relatively flat, I seldom move out of my 52/15 gear, which at an 80 cadence will move me along at approximately 21 mph. For hilly competition, I use a 13-14-15-16-19-24 rear cluster, which can get me up some extremely steep hills but still allow me close gearing for the flats between hills. For the Ironman course I used a 7-speed cluster (12-13-14-15-16-20-22), not so much for the sake of the hills, but because of the tremendous headwinds. Also, there are several long downhill opportunities where you can pick up on the competition if you don't run out of gears, so the 12-tooth cog came in handy on an infrequent basis. The single-step cogs were helpful because the winds tended to be gusty and shifting, which allowed me to gear up or down in small increments.

Riding Position

Another important consideration that creates more efficient movement is riding position. How you position yourself on the bike affects aerodynamics and the mechanical advantage of your leg muscles. The term mechanical advantage suggests that there is an optimal joint angle at which each muscle offers the greatest contractile force. If the seat position is correctly set, the muscles that work the knee and ankle will be little affected by riding position. The muscles that stand to be most affected by riding position are the powerful hip extensors. These muscles can offer the greatest torque when your upper torso assumes a more horizontal position. This position also offers the least wind resistance but at the expense of riding comfort.

Riding position is mainly altered by the position of your hands on the bars. Three different positions are generally used. Figure 6.10 illustrates these positions. Notice that in every position there is a slight bend in the elbows which lessens the stiffness in your ride. Bent elbows, especially in positions b and c allow for a more horizontal position in the back.

The aerodynamics of cycling are rather complex but play an extremely important role in cycling efficiency when speeds are in excess of 10 mph. A most interesting treatise on the subject appears in a recent *Scientific American* article (Gross, Kyle, & Malewicki, 1983). According to these authors, air resistance accounts for more than 80% of the total force acting to slow the rider at speeds higher than 18 mph. And, as shown in Figure 6.11, the work output increases exponentially as speeds increase. Notice also that the riding position offers you considerably faster speeds at the same work output. For instance, riding in the crouched racing position while exerting 0.3 horse power allows you to pedal at 22 mph, but only at 18 mph in the upright roadster position. Therefore, efficiency almost always demands precedence over riding comfort. Finally, you must evaluate the energy cost needed to pursue increases in speed.

As can be surmised from Figure 6.11 once again, the energy cost of cycling at 20 mph in the crouched racing position is 0.25 hp—a reasonable work load for a trained cyclist. Should the cyclist wish to increase the speed to 25 mph, the work output nearly doubles.

Wind resistance plays a tremendous effect on the energy cost of cycling at speeds greater than 18 mph. Because of this, you must carefully evaluate whether

Position A

Figure 6.10 Three acceptable handlebar/hand positions. Note the reduced frontal surface as the hand positions lower onto the bars.

Position B

Position C

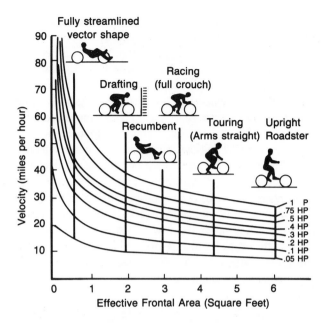

Figure 6.11 The effect of streamlining is to improve the performance of human-powered vehicles at all levels of power input. The upright roadster is the least streamlined vehicle, the vector shape the most streamlined. Drafting means to follow closely behind another vehicle, here a bicycle. A good athlete can produce 1 h.p. for about 30 sec and a healthy nonathlete for about 12 sec. They can sustain an output of .4 and .1 h.p., respectively, for about 8 hours. From "Aerodynamics of Human-Powered Land Vehicles" by A. Gross, C. Kyle, and D. Malewicki, Dec. 1983, *Scientific American*, p. 149. Reprinted by permission.

or not you can commit the greater energy demands to gain the small increases in speed. Possibly a more efficient use of your limited energy stores would be to increase your running speed instead. Here, the work required to overcome wind drag is very negligible, allowing for work to go directly into the movement.

Cycling through hills presents a new set of challenges. When pedaling uphill, it is generally best to combine a reduced gear ratio with a reduced pedal cadence. Since hills require brute power, seek out a gear that you can work using about a 70 cadence.

Two very acceptable hill-climbing positions are to pedal both in and out of the saddle. When climbing in the saddle, the position is similar to the normal riding position but with more emphasis given to the horizontal torso position. Since power is so important in executing hills, this lowered position will allow more force to be exerted by the hip extensors (see Figure 6.10c). Climbing out of the saddle allows you to use more of your body weight, but energy will be sapped if this position is maintained for an extended period of time. Climbing out of the saddle gives you the opportunity to stretch out tired muscles that have maintained the sitting position for long periods. When rides are long, this new position is a welcome change. For this position, the hands need to be placed on the brake hoods as shown in Figure 6.10b. The bike then sways slightly from side to side, but you still maintain a straight line in the direction of the ascent.

Riding downhill can provide you with a brief rest. As soon as the grade points downward, move through your gears quickly, assume an aerodynamic profile and spin out in your highest gear. Once you have topped out on your cadence, lower yourself into the bike, elbows tucked in, crank arms held horizontally to the ground and knees pulled inward. Wait out the descent and allow your body some much needed rest. This position is demonstrated in Figure 6.12.

Some comments related to the cycling position for the triathlete might be helpful at this point. Practice riding in hand-positions b and c only (see Figure 6.10). Consider saving position c for those windy stretches or for those welcomed downhills. Riding the drops for long periods will undoubtedly create a stiff, sore back that can grossly affect the run phase that follows. Trade off on positions b and c on a regular basis and save yourself some back and neck soreness.

Cycle Training for the Triathlete

The greatest formula for success in cycling is simply spending time in the saddle. Not that there aren't ways to maximize the effectiveness of your long hours,

Figure 6.12 Proper downhill aerodynamic postioning.

but the bottom line is getting accustomed to riding for long periods of time. If you have the opportunity to train on the actual competition course, you can maximize training by attempting to match your training to the demands required in the race. This applies to distance as well as terrain.

An easy trap cyclists fall into is training at mediocrity. This is where you grind out mile after mile, workout after workout, without any real improvement from your efforts. Realistically, it is very difficult to produce quality miles, day after day, without some outside help. One of the best ways to break through training mediocrity, or what some people call "garbage miles," is to ride with a local bike racing club for some of their distance training sessions. Although the way they draft off each other, attack hills, and mix up their sprint segments are not conducive to triathlon training, the change in pace is very healthy and can serve as an index of what you are truly capable of doing.

Successful cycle training and competition require a quality mix of physical and mental toughness. The cycling phase of the triathlon offers competitors a tremendous variety of excuses to justify dropping out. Flat tires and mechanical problems are the obvious, but equally lethal are the mental battles with which you are confronted when facing mile after mile of strong headwinds and/or rolling hills. Be prepared both mentally and physically for the unexpected as they will surely present themselves when the going gets tough.

Preventive Maintenance

Mechanical problems can arise at any time in both training and competing, but there are several things you can do to minimize these occurrences. The number one nemesis is the flat tire. To best minimize this problem, train on roads that are well maintained. While living in Minnesota I remember averaging at least one flat every other day because of the terrible backroads to work. High performance tires are just not built to withstand the abuse given by chuckholes, garbage on the pavement, and the like. Now I use a summer route exclusively because I know the roads so well that flats have been virtually eliminated.

Another preventive technique for flats is to clean off your tires after going through loose gravel or passing over glass. This is where cycling gloves come in handy. While in motion, lightly rub the reinforced palm over the rolling surface of the front tire. For the back tire, place the palm just behind the seat tube, lower onto the rear tire, and rub in like manner. Don't be surprised to see glass fly off when you do this. Finally, don't ride on treadless tires. Not only is this unsafe, but it's begging for flat problems.

If your bike is well maintained, tire repair is about your only concern when riding. For those who ride on clinchers, I recommend carrying one spare tube, two tire irons, and a patch kit. All this equipment can easily fit under your seat, allowing you to forget about it until the need arises. If you ride on tubulars, you only need two spares. In either case, a quarter tucked away somewhere can come in handy should you have to call for help.

Probably the next biggest concern in bike maintenance is chain-related. Chains stretch, and over time they will play havoc with the teeth on both your chainrings and rear cogs. When this happens, your $5.00 chain replacement cost is combined with another $60.00 to replace all your gears. I keep two chains on hand at all times. While I ride with one, the other is soaking in solvent, so it is clean and ready to go when it's time to switch. The time to change your chain varies with your environment, so change it if you ever get caught in rain or are confronted with windy rides. Lubricating your chain is also very important. A well-lubricated chain is perfectly silent in its function. Any chain noise whatsoever should signal you to get to work on it. Finally, when you rivet your chain back on, you must loosen up that stiff link. If you forget this measure, you will experience the frustration of a skipping chain.

Getting caught in rain presents some extra maintenance problems that go beyond the chain. Because your bike is probably made of steel, and your bearings have grease that is susceptible to dirt and water (regardless if the grease claims to be waterproof), you will need to dismantle all moving parts not containing sealed bearings. This requires some additional shop equipment, but the cost is far cheaper than replacing parts ruined because of dirt and rust. After I get caught in a rain, or two, I will dismantle my bike and let the frame dry out before reassembling. I then regrease the headset and bottom bracket, put on a freshly cleaned and lubricated chain, and clean off the rest of the bike. The total process takes me about 20 minutes to dismantle and about 45 minutes to reassemble and adjust.

Something that can't be emphasized enough is the importance of doing your own bicycle maintenance. You should be able to change a broken spoke, true a wheel, change a chain, and maintain your headset and bottom bracket. Tools to perform all these functions will cost about $20; plus there are plenty of excellent texts on the subject. Well established books such as *The Ten Speed Bicycle* by de la Rosa and Kolin (1979) or Sloan's *The New Complete Book of Bicycling* (1970) can take you through the maintenance of your entire bicycle. Other maintenance measures you should perform on a less frequent basis would be to inspect your rims for their trueness, check your brake pads for wear, and make sure your derailleurs are adjusted properly. Bicycles that are well maintained and of acceptable quality are remarkably reliable and a sheer joy to ride.

Chapter 7

The Long Run

We now focus our attention to the phase in the triathlon where skill and equipment play a small role relative to overall success. Nevertheless, running presents the triathlete with a unique set of complications, for out of all the events in the triathlon, running is the most demanding. It is the only sport in which you are required to carry your total body weight. The swimmer can float when fatigued, and the biker is given an occasional rest on downhills and tailwinds, but the runner lacks these refreshing opportunities. Even downhill running plays havoc with a fatigued body. To compound these problems even further, the run phase generally begins in a fatigued, semidehydrated state. How, then, can the competitor make the best of the run phase?

The serious triathlete can begin by training adequately for the run. Most triathletes come from a running background, and because they consider themselves established runners, run training is compromised in effort to better focus attention on the other, less familiar events. Unfortunately, this can be a costly mistake; the run in a triathlon is vastly different than the run experienced as a one-event sport. The main difference relates to the level of fatigue. In triathlons, the run phase is performed in the fatigued state almost from the onset.

Not long ago I received a letter from a 2:28 marathoner asking for some tips to improve his triathlon performance. We both had competed in a particularly long and hilly triathlon. He was quite proud of his blistering cycling phase (4th fastest), but had put in a middle-of-the-pack run performance. My cycling performance was 2 minutes slower than his, but I checked in with the fastest run of the race in spite of the vast differences between our marathon personal records (PR)s. Surely this competitor shirked run training (triathlon style) and focused his energies elsewhere.

A possible rationale behind underestimating the run phase in triathlons relates to the concept of "cross-training." Advanced by authors such as Sally Edwards (1983), Glenn Kranzley (1983), and Carol Hogan (1983), the term refers to the running improvement that one can enjoy from bicycle and swim training. As was pointed out in Chapter 4 concerning specificity of training, this cross-training rationale has no scientific foundation. A safer argument, interestingly enough, would be to suggest that run training can cross-train to improve cycling performance and even swimming performance to a small degree. Although this research may seem confusing to you, it appears that run training vastly improves the central circulatory system (heart, lungs, and vascular system) more than any other exercise except Nordic skiing. And because the central circulatory system is shared by all aerobic type exercises, improvements can be noted in exercises different from running.

Cross-training proponents quickly acknowledge that the muscles used in swimming are different from those used in running and cycling but see a commonality between cycling and running muscles. Because the leg muscles are heavily involved in both, cross-training must exist. But consider the following problems related to this idea of cross-training.

First, there is a difference in muscle fiber types required of these two sports. Costill and others (1973) observed that the distance-running movement primarily uses slow-twitch muscle fibers, whereas Gollnick and others (1973) observed that the cycling muscles use mainly the fast-twitch muscle fibers. This research suggests that even where the same muscles are used in both activities, the muscle fibers are quite different.

The second issue concerns the biomechanics of the two sports. The running movement is mainly dependent upon the two smaller gluteal muscles (gluteus medius and minimus) and one of the hamstring muscles (semitendinosus) for the forward propulsion. Help also comes from the calf muscles (gastrocnemius and soleus) at the point of push-off. However, as was shown in Chapter 6, cycling receives its power mainly from the gluteus maximus with assistance coming from the quads and the hamstrings. This suggests that the predominant muscles in the two sports being compared are not the same.

Even where muscle use does overlap from cycling to running, the range of motion and the lengths of muscles being contracted are quite different. In the cycling movement, the hip moves through a 48- to 90-degree range of motion during a complete revolution of the pedals. In running, however, the hip moves from 154 to 188 degrees at an 8 min/mile pace and 143 to 196 degrees at a 6 min/mile pace (Town, 1982).

What does all this data suggest? Basically, it means that the movements are different enough to warrant separate training programs. The muscles used are different; those that are shared in both events are used differently and call upon different fiber components of the muscles.

For the triathlete, these differences are ultimately advantageous. Imagine the level of fatigue you would experience if the same muscles were required to perform both cycling and running movements! Another advantage relates to the principles of carbohydrate loading. As suggested earlier, carbohydrate loading is muscle specific; muscles cannot share their carbohydrate reserves with other muscles having a greater need. Therefore, if the body has been adequately trained and carbohydrate loaded in both cycling and running, the bicycle phase of the triathlon, regardless of how fatiguing, will still leave the running muscles with carbohydrate reserves. This benefit would not be available if the muscles used in both sports were the same and/or used in the same way.

Running Biomechanics

Let us now focus directly on the running movement by first critiquing what is generally accepted as proper running form. Figure 7.1 illustrates this proper running form.

Foot Movement

First, note that the foot movement should initiate contact with the surface at the heel and then roll forward with a push-off coming from the toe box as is shown in Figure 7.1b. Faster running speeds will cause the heel to strike more forward and, in effect, become a flat-footed or even a midsole contact instead. Before shoes were made specifically for running, we were taught to run on our toes. This way the ankle served as a shock absorber but at the expense of premature fatigue of the calf muscles (gastrocnemius and soleus). Injuries were also commonplace with this technique. Shock absorption is best accomplished through a thick rubber cushion at the heel of the shoe and the slight bend in the knee that is maintained throughout the entire movement. Most of the running community has changed to the more accepted heel-strike movement, but occasionally I will see runners up on their toes.

Figure 7.1 Proper running form.

Stride Length

Stride length (Figure 7.1a) should be of a comfortable length and not over-exaggerated. Inefficiency, as well as hip and knee problems, can result from stride lengths being too long. Victims of an overexaggerated stride length tend to demonstrate more of a "hop" from one foot to the next, whereas good efficient runners have very little vertical movement in their stride. After all, the objective is to move forward, not upward.

A forward lean to the movement should originate from the pelvic area as shown in Figure 7.1c. This amount of lean increases as the speed of the movement increases. At an 8 mph pace, the forward lean is about 7 degrees and increases to about 9 degrees at 10 mph. A sprinter, on the other hand, has a forward lean between 12 and 15 degrees. Arms should be kept relaxed and horizontal to the ground's surface. Arms should definitely move in cooperation with the trunk so that the upper body counterrotates the movement of the lower body. Fatigued runners tend to raise and to tighten the shoulders which defeats this function. Make sure the shoulders remain relaxed by occasionally shaking them out, especially when fatigue sets in.

The biomechanical changes that allow for increases in speed are mainly concerned with stride length and stride rate. Sinning and Foreseyth (1970), in their biomechanical analysis of running form at different speeds, suggest that increases in speed at the lower rates occurs mainly by an increase in stride length. As speed increases, stride rate also increases but becomes the predominant factor in increasing speed when the runner approaches 15 mph. Changes in stride length occur mainly from a increase in hip flexion which, in effect, causes you to lower yourself into the stride. When it comes to determining one's optimal stride, the work of Hogberg (1952) demonstrated greatest efficiency to be an individual matter. The most efficient stride length was the one in which the individual runner felt most comfortable. These data suggest that increases in running speed should not be attempted by forcing biomechanical changes on yourself, but by merely allowing the necessary changes to occur naturally.

Fatigue Running

Running when fatigued creates a new set of complications that deserves investigation. Fatigue running lacks the smooth, fluid motion that looks and feels so natural. The body becomes more vertical, with little effort to stay relaxed. But the real problem lies with the legs which resort to a shorter stride and a minimal bend in the knee. The stiff knee probably serves as protection against buckling under the fatigue. Also, the feet tend to strike very flat-footed with little effort extended toward pushing off with the ankle at the end of the stride (see Figure 7.1b).

Based on these observations, much of your training runs should include running in the fatigued condition. Benefits to this type of training are two-fold. First, you will condition your body to burn fat stores more effectively. Regardless of the amount of carbohydrates your body can store, you still rely on fats to provide energy in a big way. If your training program does not allow you to train while fatigued, fat utilization will not be effectively developed. Second, fatigue training will allow your body to adapt or develop a training effect to the fatigue experience. In other words, you can train your body to tolerate fatigue.

Fatigue Training

Two cautions should be mentioned when training while fatigued. First, you should not begin fatigue training until your running movement is well developed, and the distances required of you in competition are within your capabilities. A very real possibility associated with fatigue training is injury, especially at the knees and hips. Second, fatigue training should be only an occasional, not a regular part of your training program. Running under these conditions can be very frustrating and discouraging, tolerated by most only on an infrequent basis. (Fatigue training about twice weekly is enough for me.)

Let us then consider several ways to train while fatigued. Probably the best way is to combine cycling and running in a similar manner to the real triathlon experience. As soon as you finish a long bike ride, dismount, quickly jump into your running gear, and head out. Your first few attempts at this experience may take you only a mile down the road before you "throw in the towel," but soon you will move out of this prolonged adjustment phase. The reason you feel this immediate fatigue is because of the lactic acid which is being rapidly developed. Realize that all available blood is being directed into the muscles used in cycling. When you quickly move into the new and unfamiliar experience of running, these new muscles are void of adequate circulation and must rely on energy to be provided anaerobically until the blood can be rerouted into the needy muscles. Energy produced this way will create the overwhelming sense of fatigue. This job of rerouting the blood supply, just like any other physical task, can be efficiently developed through training in such a manner.

The second way to train under fatigued conditions is, of course, by running long slow distances. Certainly many of you have experienced fatigue when training in this manner and realize that the experience is as much mental as it is physical. I consider this fatigue training valuable mainly for the run phase where the accumulation of all previous work expended in swimming and cycling is realized.

Equipment

About all that deserves comment when considering equipment needs for run training is the type and quality of running shoes. It hasn't been that long since we have had running shoes readily available for purchase. Back in the mid 60s our high school track team had to travel 25 miles to buy shoes, and the town we lived in had a population of 160,000! Once we narrowed our decision down to the need for training flats, racing flats, or track spikes, the choices were limited to two or three models. Selection between brands was unheard of! Now, the development of running shoes has advanced to accommodate a variety of differences among runners. We have overpronator shoes, heel striker shoes, midsole striker shoes, extra cushioned shoes, shoes promoting stability, and others.

Allow me to make a few generalizations that might help you when choosing among all the specialized shoes that are on the market. You should probably start by determining whether or not you overpronate when running. Figure 7.2 shows the right foot pronating excessively both in and out of the shoe.

Observe your heel strike when walking and running, both in and out of your shoes. Overpronators tend to show wear on the inside of the heel strike area instead of the outside, which demonstrates normal wear. The normal wear of a running shoe should run from the outside of the heel strike area across the center of the midsole and then show wear on the forward area of the toe box. If you suspect that you overpronate, have it confirmed by an expert and then purchase shoes to compensate.

Another generalization that can be safely made has to do with comparing a cushioned shoe design to one promoting stability. Many manufacturers produce shoes that feel like you're walking on clouds because that is what impresses the consumer. Unfortunately, the trade-off to this luxury is a very unstable shoe. The runner using soft-soled shoes will quickly start to roll out of the built-in heel cup, resulting in a loss of stability at the ankle. Because of this, the knee must compensate by serving as the stabilizing joint in the leg. This function is poorly performed at the knee and sharp pains often infiltrate the knee. Carefully avoid shoes that sacrifice stability for added cushion. Below is a list of additional concerns to consider when purchasing shoes.

1. Most importantly, the shoe must fit properly and feel comfortable. Blisters will result from a shoe that is too tight or too loose. The toes should be allowed free movement with little or no friction.

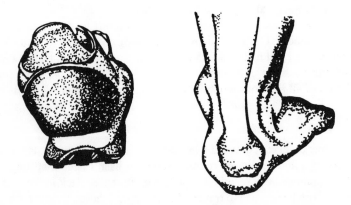

Figure 7.2 Pronation of the right foot in and out of the shoe.

2. Shoes must be properly padded to cushion shock. This must be noted especially where the heel strike occurs. Some racing flats compromise in this area.

3. Make sure the midsole of the shoe bends easily. A flexible midsole helps prevent Achilles tendon problems.

4. Check the shoes from the back and make sure they are aligned properly and not tilted to one side. Even brand new shoes can come from the factory with serious imbalances due to improper gluing.

5. Pick a slightly larger shoe over a slightly smaller one to compensate for foot swelling when running.

6. Shoe sizes vary from brand to brand and even within brands themselves. Most shoes are geared for a D width. Some brands run narrow, some wide. If you have a foot drastically different than a D width, consider trying a different brand as opposed to selecting a different size simply because of a width problem.

7. Finally, if after a brief break-in period your shoes are still causing feet and leg problems, quit wearing them! Better to sacrifice the shoe than to sacrifice the legs. Attempt to negotiate with the shoe salesman for an exchange.

Chapter 8

Seven Days To Go

When the body is in training, the muscles remain in a constant state of repair, and the body's carbohydrate stores are always in a semidepleted state. Both of these conditions are necessary if increases in strength and endurance are to occur (overload principle). Let me add that when carbohydrate stores are constantly being depleted, they, too, make adaptations to take on greater reserves. Muscle hypertrophy (enlargement) and muscle strength develop most effectively when the body is in a semifatigued state. But because optimal performance cannot be achieved when the body is not fully recovered, the triathlete must decide when training must diminish, and full recovery—physically, mentally, and nutritionally—must take precedence. Therefore, the purpose of this chapter is to first consider how to enter into a state of optimal physical repair and then how to maximize carbohydrate stores.

Anywhere from 5 to 7 days before the big day of competition, you will need to enter into a state of physical and nutritional depletion. Allowing more than a week places you in jeopardy of entering into the detraining process, and when performed with fewer than 5 days before the race, will not allow for full recovery.

Consider the depletion workout as your grand finale of training, for what remains should be minimal training and maximal eating. Probably the most effective depletion workout would be to replicate as closely as possible the demands expected of you on race day. Not only will you deplete the carbohydrate stores in the muscles needed for competition, but you will also have the added confidence of knowing that you can go the distance. This effort may be unrealistic, however, especially if you are competing in events requiring Ironman distances. A very effective alternative would be to deplete by exercising at high intensities in all three events. Figure 8.1 presents some muscle glycogen depletion data while cycling at different intensities.

Although exercising at 75% of maximum effort lasted for a shorter duration, the carbohydrate depletion was most effective. Regardless of the technique you choose for depletion purposes, you must expose yourself to a high level of fatigue by the time your workout is completed.

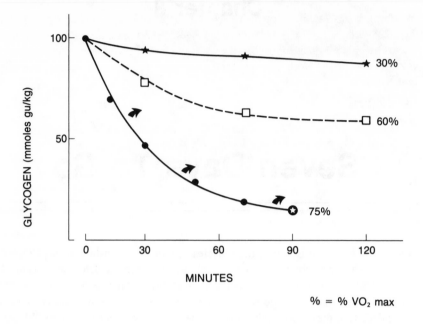

Figure 8.1 Rate of muscle glycogen depletion at different cycling intensities. From *Ergogenic Aids in Sport* (p. 6) by W. Sherman, 1983, Champaign, IL: Human Kinetics Publishers, Inc. Reprinted by permission.

The purpose of fatiguing the body is first to initiate carbohydrate depletion and, second, to begin the final muscle rebuilding stage. As was mentioned previously, glycogen supercompensation is a very specific process. If you fail to adequately deplete all the carbohydrate stores in the muscles required of you in competition, your depletion effort will be compromised. Skeletal muscle is the most important site for glycogen storage, but this fuel is not free to move out of the muscle in which it is being stored. The only general distribution center for carbohydrates is the liver, but its stores are very limited. Any muscle that is not adequately depleted and later supercompensated could possibly call upon liver glycogen stores to provide fuel for contraction. However, this could eventually prove lethal; liver glycogen needs to be reserved as fuel for nervous tissue function. What final word can we give? Simple. Deplete the swimming muscles by swimming, and do exactly the same for cycling and running. That's all there is to it.

Carbohydrate Loading

Carbohydrate loading was introduced by Swedish researchers in the late 1960s. This technique consisted of a depletion phase (two consecutive days of exhaustive exercise), a restricted carbohydrate diet for the next 3 days, and then a diet high in carbohydrates for the remainder of the week. Although this technique still produces the greatest quantity of stored muscle glycogen, some severe consequences may be associated with this regimen. Sherman (1983) lists several possible complications:

> The 3 days of low carbohydrate diet leads to hypoglycemia and associated nausea, fatigue, dizziness, and irritability; Two bouts of exhaustive exercise during the week prior to an important competition might result in injury and disrupt tapering for the event; A diet containing 95% carbohydrates is not a practical diet. Since the body is not used to a week of such radical dieting, problems such as diarrhea and its associated mineral and water losses can and often result.

Because of these common problems, other glycogen supercompensation techniques have been developed which still demonstrate high muscle glycogen loading but with less drastic diet and exercise regimens. The technique was developed by Sherman (1980) and Sherman and others (1981) which consisted of a single day's depletion workout 7 days before competition. The first 3 days of dieting was a mixed diet containing 50% carbohydrates, followed by 3 days of a 70% carbohydrate diet. The accelerated carbohydrate diet totaled 500-600g of carbohydrates per day, or 2,000 to 2,400 Kcal of carbohydrates. Added to the carbohydrates were an additional 600 to 700 Kcals coming from fat and protein consumption.

The training that followed the depletion workout was at 40% duration of the depletion workout for Days 2 and 3, and 20% of the depletion days exercise duration for Days 4 and 5 with Day 6 serving as a rest day before the competition. Training intensity was at race pace. Figure 8.2 compares the Swedish classical regimen to the "modified" program proposed by Sherman. Note that muscle glycogen storage levels resulting from the modified technique were nearly identical to that of the radical diet and exercise technique originally proposed.

A second alternative to the conventional carbo-loading technique is in essence no alternate diet and exercise program at all. Costill and others (1981) observed that extremely high levels of muscle glycogen could be stored in exercising muscles without undergoing a major depletion workout or diet manipulation. Their research indicated that as long as exercise remained sufficient to stimulate development of the chemicals necessary to produce glycogen, the desired end-result would occur if sufficient carbohydrates were being consumed. Sherman, in the book *Ergogenic Aids in Sport* (1983) states:

> It is feasible, therefore, that no 'special' regimen of muscle glycogen supercompensation is necessary in well-trained runners, and it may be necessary to think of muscle glycogen levels as being 'some degree of full' rather than as supercompensated or nonsupercompensated.

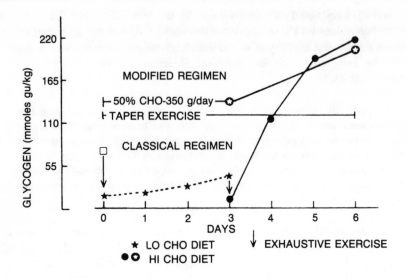

Figure 8.2 Level of carbohydrate supercompensation attained by various techniques. From *Ergogenic Aids in Sport* (p. 14) by W. Sherman, 1983, Champaign, IL: Human Kinetics Publishers, Inc. Reprinted by permission.

When developing your next plan for carbohydrate loading, consider the alternatives in light of the risks associated with the original, more drastic, technique.

The Training Taper

On several occasions the term "taper" or "training taper" was mentioned. This suggests a reduction in training intensity and duration prior to the major competition. The purpose of the taper is to allow for maximum physical healing, mental and emotional preparation, and optimal storage of fuels.

When training is ongoing, the microstructure of skeletal muscle remains in a constant state of degradation and rebuilding. This constant tearing down and repairing is a normal and preferred phenomenon: skeletal muscle rebuilds to greater capacities than previous levels, thus, meeting the demands placed on them in the future. Although these developments wonderfully represent the body's remarkable ability to adapt, there is risk involved when abused. Whenever the body is in a state of repair, the chances of muscle and connective tissue injury is increased. Those who neglect to give the body adequate time and nutrition for the repair process to occur may eventually fall prey to injury and illness. Sooner or later, the body will get the rest it needs. Full recovery should be the main objective for the taper period.

Research has shown that this process of recovery is best performed through what is called "active recovery." The implication here is that some activity continues during this recovery period so that (a) optimal production of chemicals (enzymes) needed to process the energy nutrients continues; (b) the process of detraining does not begin; (c) blood vessels in the skeletal muscles remain optimaly dilated to receive maximum blood flow; and (d) muscle and joint stiffness, a natural response to detraining does not occur. In addition, it has been shown that healing occurs quicker and with greater strength when exercising as opposed to receiving a resting recovery (Tipton, 1975). This is plausible, since exercise brings more blood—the healing element of the body—into the injury site.

Nutritionally, the body requires time to refuel the depleted storage sites and to optimally resynthesize the chemicals that build up and break down the fats, carbohydrates, and proteins our exercising muscles desperately need. "Topping off" the energy storage sites is probably best accomplished by at least one day of complete rest before competition.

From a psychological and emotional perspective, the taper week should allow you to rebound from the mental slump often associated with long, hard training. Thoughts should no longer focus on past training successes and failures, but should be on that final task—the conclusion of all you have been training for.

Sleep

A common thread that runs through the emotional/psychological, nutritional, and physical person is the need for proper sleep. As the big day approaches, this important commodity tends to be minimized when, in fact, the need is greatest. If you sense that your anxiety level is quite high toward the end of a training taper, consider taking an over-the-counter sleeping pill 2 nights before the race. Sleeping pills on the eve of the race are not recommended for fear of decreasing performance due to the residual chemical agents that may remain in the body.

The Pregame Meal

The pregame meal represents one of those sociological phenomenon that has changed in obedience to the recommendations of research. So often sport scientists reveal incorrect practices or better ways of doing things but can never implement their ideas because of unbending sociological practices. When I was in high school, the pregame meal always consisted of steak and associated favorites, for eating steak was an issue of self-esteem. To receive anything less suggested that either the athlete wasn't important or that the contest was not important. Further rationale for this meal focused on the mindset that protein meant strength—the important ingredient for the upcoming competition. Little did the coaches realize that protein is important only in relatively small quantities and that the high protein, high-fat meal is so costly to digest! Meals of this nature require approximately 30% of all calories consumed to go toward digestion.

Maybe it was the positive way in which promoters introduced the concept of carbohydrate-loading parties, but whatever it was, the concept was nutritionally correct. Even so, the social pressure to make food tasty requires supplementing the carbohydrates with plenty of fat. The prudent athlete who sees performance more important than satiety will avoid fat and protein-oriented pregame foods.

A marvelous idea from the Hawaii Ironman sponsors is to hold the carbo-loading party 2 nights prior to the race. Not only is this nutritionally sound, but it also helps to keep anxiety levels under control. Also, eating a large meal the night before the race is unwise because the food residue will not clear the body in that short a period.

Other Taper Week Concerns

During your taper week, you are probably going to find extra time on your hands. For some, cutting back on training time to 40%, could offer an extra 3 or 4 hours in the day for other concerns. Sometimes idleness creates anxiety, so you will no doubt be looking to finalize some triathlon-related matters. Two tasks with which you must deal during the taper week are bike maintenance and course familiarization.

Since you are not allowed maintenance support after the gun sounds, you must troubleshoot everything possible ahead of time. I recommend that all parts with bearings be dismantled, inspected for pitting or excessive wear, regreased, and then reassembled. Inspect all cables for fraying or rust. Go over spoke tension and wheel trueness thoroughly. Perform this work early enough in your taper week so that you can road check all adjustments at least twice.

Your next step, and certainly the most crucial, is to inspect and install your best tires. Most competitors have a set of tires that are used strictly for racing. Before installing them, inspect the entire surface of the tire for any pieces of glass or rock embedded deep enough into the rubber to go unnoticed, though not deep enough to puncture the tube. These lethal specks can eventually break through without warning.

The second prerace task is to become familiar with the race course. I have heard competitors say they prefer not to know the course ahead of time, which in my estimation is like burying your head in the sand. Much of your race strategy depends on being familiar with the course because the way you distribute your energy depends on the course characteristics. As you review the course, make sure that your bike is adequately geared for the hills and that you know the route. Local triathlons are notorious for assuming that each competitor knows the route, and often neglecting to provide course marshals at key intersections.

Chapter 9

Race Day

The vast majority of this day's outcome has already been determined. If you trained well, if your taper and carbohydrate loading were done correctly, and if your equipment has been well-cared for, you will almost certainly perform up to your expectations. Obviously, your performance will require a tremendous amount of work plus a dose of good fortune at some key places along the way. In this chapter I will consider all phases of race day in hopes that you will optimize the controllable factors and be better prepared for the unexpected.

Personalized Race Strategy

Well before entering the water you should have developed a race strategy based on your personal strengths and weaknesses. One of the most interesting aspects of the triathlon is that the competition is so unpredictable. The first person out of the water, for instance, may end up being a back-of-the-pack hacker by the race's end. Most triathlons now publicize the best performances in each of the three events. Athletes know this, and many treat the triathlon as a single event in hopes of recognition where they are strongest, knowing they will never finish high in the overall standings. Therefore, don't be discouraged if someone zips by, only to be overcome by you later in the race.

Because of these unique race features, I strongly suggest that prudent triathletes know and go their own pace. Those who get caught up in the surrounding competition run a high risk of running out of energy supplies before the demands of the competition are met. The rationale for this recommendation is founded upon the need to conserve energy. The very nature of the triathlon requires you to maintain a steady pace and to be patient.

Fluid and Fuel Replacement

Prior to the actual race, you need to develop a strategy for dealing with the two biggest physiological problems associated with endurance competition: dehydration and depletion of fuel reserves. Let us look at these two concerns in relationship with each other because they are somewhat contradictory. Whenever you consume sugar-based liquids, you will experience a delay in gastric emptying. In other words, sugars, regardless of type, will impede the rate at which water is moved out of the stomach and made available for metabolic needs (Costill & Fink, 1974). Consequently, when the need for fluid replacement is critical (as in dehydration conditions), consume only water. If the day is cool and dehydration is of little concern, you can consume sugar-based drinks in hopes of adding some calories to the fuel reserves. In terms of surviving the heat, fluid replacement takes precedence over fuel replacement. A common sense rule of thumb is to focus on the problem of dehydration when conditions are hot and to focus on glucose replenishment when dehydration is not a problem.

Even if the conditions are hot, food can and should be consumed during the bike phase. Liquid-based foods such as oranges, or a 50/50 mix of cola and water are excellent to consume on the bike. Bananas are also popular because they are easy to eat, easy to digest, and are high in water, carbohydrates, and potassium. Although sandwiches are often available on longer triathlons, you need to experiment with these before race day. Sandwiches are very difficult to eat on a hot day because they require so much saliva to initiate digestion, and this product is in low supply when you are hot and dry.

Once you are into the run phase, your best bet is probably to stick with consuming water only. The concern here is twofold: First, great amounts of sweat are produced during the run. Unlike the bike phase where the wind aids in cooling, running requires more evaporative cooling, a process requiring extra body water. Second, energy demands are greatest in the run phase. More blood, therefore, must be distributed to the muscles in need instead of some being shunted to the gut for fuel digestion. Finally, even under the most optimal conditions, it still takes 20 to 30 minutes from the time carbohydrates enter the stomach to reach the muscles in need. If you feel a need for fuel replacement in the run phase, realize that commercial preparations such as Gatorade, Instant Replay, or Take-Five contain 5% glucose and will significantly retard the replacement of lost fluids during exercise in the heat.

McArdle, Katch, and Katch (1981) offer these recommendations related to water replacement:

> Studies of fluid absorption indicate that cold fluids (5 degrees C; 41 degrees F) are emptied from the stomach at a significantly faster rate than fluids at body temperature. The volume of fluid in the stomach is also of importance because gastric emptying speeds up for each 100 ml increase in gastric volume up to 600 ml. A volume of about 250 ml (8.5 oz) ingested at 10- to 15-minute intervals is probably a realistic goal because larger volumes tend to produce feelings of a 'full stomach.' Thus, to obtain a high rate of fluid absorption, the stomach should remain partially filled and the fluid ingested should be relatively cold.

Racing Garb

Let us next consider clothing and footwear needs for the actual race. Generally, the swim phase requires only a suit, cap, and goggles. Nylon suits have less drag in the water than cotton or wool suits. Also, the tighter the fit, the less the resistance. Race officials often require swim caps, as they aid in rescue attempts. Caps also serve to cut down on drag created by loose hair and can conserve valuable heat lost through the head in hypothermic water conditions. Goggles are essential in saltwater and in chlorinated water but can sometimes be omitted in shorter, freshwater swims. Goggles leak, fog up, and often become uncomfortable; so if you intend to use goggles in your race, wear them in practice. This way, any personal problems you might have with them are rectified in advance.

What you wear for the rest of the race depends on several concerns. If the race is very short, you would probably benefit from wearing a combination swim, cycling, and running suit. These outfits are called triathlon suits and can save you a few minutes in changing during transitions. As a swim suit, they offer slightly more drag than the traditional wear but might better insulate the body in hypothermic conditions. As far as riding shorts, the extra padding is usually cotton since chamois liners absorb and retain the water from the swim phase. These cotton liners are thin, providing less padding between you and the bike seat. As a running suit, these three-in-one outfits are tighter than traditional running shorts. I feel these triathlon suits have greatest value when the bike and run phases take less than an hour each.

When considering longer races, most prefer the traditional bike and running wear. Why? Long rides will inevitably create saddle soreness. When this happens, you find yourself moving around on the saddle, standing up while riding, and so on. A well-padded pair of riding shorts will aid greatly in delaying this discomfort. Something else to consider is the need to urinate and/or void feces during longer races. One-piece suits have an obvious disadvantage here. In addition, skintight material is restrictive and annoying when running.

For shorter races, a possible alternative to the triathlon suit is to wear running shorts under your cycling shorts. When you finish the bike phase, simply peel off the first layer, and, you are dressed for the run!

Another decision you must make before race time is whether or not to use cycling shoes. Using cycling shoes can definitely improve cycling stroke mechanics, creating a more efficient distribution of energy. But the time saved by wearing cycling shoes may not make up for the time lost when changing from cycling to running shoes in shorter races. For short triathlons, consider cycling in your running shoes if the width of your shoes permits unrestricted pedal movement. Be cautious about cycling in running shoes with soft or thin soles as they may numb your feet. Hilly triathlons, regardless of length, might be better executed with cycling shoes. A possible rule of thumb might be to consider using cycling shoes if the bike phase of the triathlon is hilly or is expected to last an hour or more. Regardless of footware, using lace locks on all shoes will save you from having to tie your shoes.

Finally, choose the color of your sports clothing in light of typical race day temperature. If the race is expected to be hot, light-colored cotton or nylon clothing will offer the greatest cooling. If the race is expected to be cold (which is seldom the case), layered dark-colored clothing is the preferred choice. As the temperature heats up or as you heat up, the layers can be pealed off whenever appropriate.

Race Day

Normally the first order of the day is to check in and have your race number marked on your upper arms and front thighs. You will probably need to pin race numbers on your cycling and running clothing, and secure your number somewhere on the bicycle. Very likely, the prerace jitters will be in full blossom during this time, so remember to maintain your prerace strategy. Avoid any temptation to feel inferior because competitors have better physiques or better bicycles. Remember, your goals like everyone else's are highly personal and are not to be compared with others.

You may find it helpful to ease doubt and anxiety by taking a little longer time to warm up. If your bike is not already impounded, a few easy miles on flat terrain can serve as an excellent release. Jogging a mile or so is a good substitute when the bike is unavailable. Dave Scott, the four-time Ironman champion, was reported to have biked 10 miles the morning of his successful October '82 race. Whatever warming up you do, however, leave the swim warm-up for last.

Your swim preparation should begin about 30 minutes prior to the start. This allows for full recovery but will still maintain good vascularization in the swim muscles. During the swim preparation, finalize all cap and goggle adjustments.

Racing Tips

Even in the most organized and supervised races, certain problems are bound to occur. These "surprises" can be frustrating and even traumatic. Your ability to react properly may well spare you from race withdrawal!

I will never forget my experience in a Midwest USTS triathlon where the crowded swimming conditions were more than I had bargained for. After about 10 minutes of being kicked and pounded from all sides, my thoughts were not of performance but only of survival. When I finally completed the swim, I was in such a state of physical and emotional exhaustion that the rest of the race was severely affected. So let us attempt to investigate potential problem areas in hopes of avoiding some race trauma.

Swim Phase

Swim starts will vary with each triathlon. The United States Triathlon Series (USTS), for example, generally uses a mass start technique. All swimmers, regardless of ability, start at the same time. This type of start offers both the competitors and spectators the benefit of knowing how they stand against the competition. The first to finish is the absolute winner, but this type of start creates a crowded swim condition.

Mass starts require you to self-seed. What this means is that the best swimmers should move to the front, poorest swimmers to the back, and intermediate swimmers should appropriately position themselves between these extremes. Please yield to this advice, even if it costs you a few seconds in your overall finish time. Slow swimmers ahead of faster ones stand an excellent chance of having competitors actually swim right up their backs!

Local triathlons usually attract a less intense group of competitors and often start people in groups according to ability or age. These groupings may be sent out at 1- to 10-minute intervals with finish times adjusted according to the starting delays. Seldom do you have the crowded conditions and consequent problems with this type of start, but it is difficult to see how the race is developing. Please consider entering some local triathlons with this type of start experience before attempting races with the more difficult mass starts.

As you begin the swim, concentrate on going straight and maintaining proper stroke mechanics. It is inevitable that other competitors will interrupt your kick and your arm stroke. But realize that they, too, are struggling for available water space and not intentionally breaking up your stroke.

In the 1983 Ironman, I even had my goggles knocked ajar and that could have created tremendous trauma within me. Instead, I continued swimming with one eye closed until I sensed that trailing swimmers were temporarily clear: I momentarily paused, readjusted my lens and continued on.

On the more positive side of the swim phase, look for opportunities to draft-off other swimmers. This technique is similar to bicycle drafting and can reduce your work output by as much as 30%! Also, if you find yourself getting fatigued, switch to an alternate stroke, but only as a last resort. The stroke with which you have trained will always be most efficient and should be used as long as possible.

Toward the end of the swim phase, some triathletes recommend switching to a backstroke or breaststroke movement in order to avoid cramps and to prepare the leg muscles for cycling. If you kick hard in your front crawl stroke, this advice is probably sound; but if you rely very little on the kick phase for propulsion, cramping is highly unlikely and your legs should be plenty loose for the cycling movement.

Swim to Bike Transition

Physiologically, you should find the change from swimming to running quite feasible. The upper body, fatigued from the swim, can now rest while exercise responsibilities are delegated to the legs in cycling. Changing of clothes, however, can be hectic and confusing. Oftentimes changing tents are not available, assistance not allowed, and your bike far removed from the changing area. Remain calm and alert but be thorough. Tie your shoes carefully, make sure your shorts are not on backwards, and take time to put on riding gloves before mounting; in other words, dress right the first time. Problems such as catching shoestrings in your chain or crashing while putting on gloves are simply not worth risking over the few seconds saved from a hasty transition.

Bike Phase

At the start of the bike phase, a wise triathlete will begin using a moderate pedal cadence with minimal resistance. This technique will best trigger the aerobic energy system into action and aid in injury prevention.

If your race is expected to draw a large crowd, look for pedestrians, children, and even dogs crossing the street and into your path. In the 1983 Hawaii Ironman, a competitor hit someone crossing the street, was knocked unconscious, and was eliminated from the competition. Be prepared for problems such as these whenever crowds are gathered. Once the viewing crowd has passed, settle into a comfortable riding position, for the cycling phase in triathlons is often quite long. Before you get too comfortable, however, realize that there is another crowd you need to confront for the remainder of the race. I speak here of slower cyclists who can fall into your path quite abruptly and actually cause a crash. In competition, eyes need to be continually focused on the bicycle traffic ahead.

Another congested area that requires your attention is aid stations. Make sure that your approach is clear of other cyclists when you approach such areas. When seeking food or drink, shout well in advance, and even point to your intended exchange person. Aid stations, because of their congestion, are another great threat to crashes.

I could continue describing other possible crash situations, but crashes are not the major concern among triathletes. The vast majority of contestants fear flat tires and mechanical failures the most. Ironically, the flat tire is probably more psychologically draining than anything else, because in reality, a person well-rehearsed in changing flats can do so in 3 to 4 minutes. This time period can even be cut in half by using an aerosol inflator such as Quick Fill. In any event, the victim sees so many competitors whizzing by during this down time that his or her competitive flame blows out in protest. Keep in mind that seldom does this brief pause significantly effect the final outcome of the race. Most triathlons are won by several minutes with the rest of the field spread out for hours! On the positive side of this dilemma, consider the delay as a rest allowing you to urinate if necessary. The worst thing would be to give up when so much of the race is yet to come.

I am continually amazed by how simple the mechanics of a bike are, but how unpredictable the mechanical failures can be. You can have the best, well-maintained equipment, but still experience mechanical failure. World famous cyclist John Howard dropped out of the 1983 Hawaii Ironman because of bike failure. You must be willing to accept this problem as part of the cycling experience.

The contestant cannot be equipped for every possible mishap because the problems are too varied. The best protection, therefore, is prevention. Double-check all bolts, screws, and adjustments during your taper week and go prepared to merely change flats. Attempting to intercept other mechanical problems is just too unpredictable.

Changing weather conditions often catch a competitor off-guard and can create havoc on one's prerace plans. Whether it is rain, tremendous head winds, or blazing heat, many competitors will use these environmental problems as excuses for a poor showing. Remember that these conditions are the same for everyone competing, and simply alter your race plans accordingly. If you can maintain high spirits during these times, then inclement weather will almost always work to your advantage. Poor weather may slow down your finish time, but don't be surprised to find your finish place higher than expected.

On longer bike phases such as an Ironman distances, inevitably you will get sore while riding. The most common places are buttocks, back, neck, and hands. The degree of soreness is directly related to the success of your bike training program. But even highly trained cyclists get sore, so make a few position changes during your ride. Consider riding out of the saddle when confronting some of the uphills as a good way to temporarily relieve soreness. with tail winds and downhills, accelerate to high speeds and then coast in a tucked position. Not only does this rest help with soreness, but it is efficient as well.

Finally, when you approach the finish of the bike phase, focus your thoughts to running instead of showing off with a strong bike finish. The run preparation actually begins on the bike by reducing the pedal torque to create a smoother, less-intense cycling spin. When you finally dismount, your legs may cooperate unpredictably, so be careful not to fall or slip while walking on your cycling shoes.

Bike to Run Transition

This transition, unlike the previous one, presents some real challenges physiologically; changing clothes, however, is much easier. Even with this in mind, I am continually amused by how much emphasis authors and competitors place on the techniques to speed up the changing process. Competitors are often seen taking off their jerseys while still cycling at high speeds into the transition area!

The bike/run transition area has to be the most dangerous place in the race. The scene inevitably consists of cyclists sprinting to the finish area, of runners emerging onto the running course, of officials checking numbers and finish times, and of all the spectators lining the course. USTS races will even have competitors finishing the run with all these other activities still going on.

There are, however, several ways to speed up your change without endangering yourself or others. While still on the bike, zip down the jersey and untie your left shoe. Refrain from untying your right shoe until the stopping point is nearby because the shoe strings can easily get caught in the chain. Once you begin coasting to a stop, remove your feet from the shoes and dismount in bare feet with the shoes still in the toe straps. Peel off your riding shorts to expose running shorts or bare bottom (depending on the duration of the bike phase). Once you are clothed, on go the shoes, off goes the helmet, and onto the run course with jersey in hand. If you have friends located on the course, you might consider removing your gloves after you get into the run and simply hand them off as you pass by. Consider carrying your running jersey until you are clear of the crowds and then safely putting it on while still in motion.

More important than all Clark Kent-changing techniques are the physiological concerns associated with the bike-to-run transition. This transition area is where injury and lactic acid accumulation is most susceptible. After your body has been shaped into the familiar riding position for such a long time, the more upright posture needed in running serves as a welcome relief, but it must be executed gingerly. Expect the leg muscles to have difficulty in supporting your body weight. Realize, also, that your leg muscles are receiving blood mainly in the cycling muscles and not in the running muscles. To dash off as if you have properly warmed up for running will only expose you to undue risk of muscle and tendon injury and load your running muscles with lactic acid. So be prepared to run as if you are without knees and begin at a slow pace until blood is rerouted into the newly called-upon muscles.

The Run Phase

This phase of the race has the greatest potential of success or failure depending on your level of conditioning and on how well you survived the bike phase. Success is almost assured if you have effectively trained by the fatigue run-training technique suggested in Chapter 7. If properly trained, your body will be accustomed to the unusual running form, to a slower pace, and to the need to support your total weight. People who train inadequately for the run phase carry the risk of premature carbohydrate depletion and premature exhaustion. Assuming you are well trained for this phase of the triathlon, let us then consider the problem areas you might encounter during the run.

Probably the biggest concern in the run phase is dehydration. People tend to be so afraid of stomach cramps resulting from fluids bouncing around in the stomach that they dehydrate. Make sure you drink at every aid station and try to drink plenty. I might suggest getting a full cup of ice water at each station, drink about half of the cup, and then fold the top of the cup so the valuable water is sealed off. Carry this cup like a lunch bucket and take intermittent sips until the cup is empty. This system allows you to drink on a nearly continual basis and without the need to consume in large gulps.

If sponges are offered at the aid stations, don't let them get your socks and shoes wet as this will result in blistered feet. Food is usually available at run aid stations but avoid eating at the risk of side aches and the need to keep blood in the exercising muscles instead of in the gut for digestion purposes.

Knowing how much fuel is in reserve for the run phase is impossible to estimate, so make every effort to run efficiently. Stick to your training pace, don't get caught up in the competition, and make all irrational moves only when the finish line is in sight. If you ever find yourself confronting "the wall," quickly consume some simple sugar foods such as orange sections, or pop, and temporarily back off your pace until the symptoms subside.

Chapter 10

The Ironman Triathlon World Championships

As if it had happened yesterday, I remember making my final turn onto Alii Drive for those last 700 yards toward the finish of the 1983 Ironman Triathlon World Championship. With each step, the crowd thickened, and words became indistinguishable as cheers blended into jubilant noise. Well in advance "No. 999, Glenn Town, Exercise Physiologist from Wheaton, Illinois," was announced to everyone. By now, I was being carried by the enthusiasm of this enormous crowd! The finish, with its finishers' lay and packet of awards, all added to reinforce the reality of what it meant to be an Ironman! For me, it was a dream born into reality with heavy doses of intense physical preparation, study, sacrifice, and emotion lodged in-between.

I believe it is safe to assume that the majority of triathlon competitors with even the slightest bit of passion toward their sport hold at least a remote aspiration of one day competing in the grandaddy of all triathlons—the Hawaii Ironman. For some, their dream will materialize. Others may be accepted or even start the race but never actually experience those last 700 yards down Alii Drive. But for most, the Ironman will get only as close as the various media covering the famed event will allow.

The purpose of this chapter is to help you assess your potential in becoming an Ironman. As you journey the course through the following pages and illustrations, and as I guide you in counting the cost related to training, funding, and competing, I trust that you will be able to fuel your dream more realistically. I hope that those of you for whom the cost is too great will still enjoy my account of the race.

The road to Ironman begins several years in advance. Your triathlon background should expose you to progressively longer races in order to confirm your ability to complete the distances Ironman demands. Because this race now has stiff qualifiers, your portfolio of past performances may require several years of effort to provide you with necessary requisites.

The necessary paperwork is the first step to Ironman for everyone. Request application forms no later than February or early March as application requests must be received by March 15. Written requests should be sent to:

Ironman Triathlon World Championship
1100 Ward Ave., Suite 815
Honolulu, Hawaii 96814

Since applications now exceed acceptances, the only sure way of getting accepted is by qualifying in 1 of 3 categories. Category 1 considers qualifying finish times from previous Ironman races and are as follows:

Table 10.1   Qualifying Finish Times from Previous Ironman Races

Men		Women	
18-34	11:45:00	18-29	12:00:00
35-39	12:15:00	30-34	12:45:00
40-44	12:45:00	35-39	13:15:00
45-49	13:00:00	40-44	14:00:00
50-54	13:30:00	45-49	14:30:00
55-59	14:15:00	50 +	17:00:00
60 +	16:15:00		

Category 2 gives priority to a limited number of foreign contestants and does not apply to American citizens visiting, working, or stationed in foreign countries.

Category 3 gives those who fail to qualify in any of the first two categories a chance for acceptance through a lottery. Here, applicants are grouped by age, and then drawn at random to allow equal distribution among the various age groups. Approximately 300 applicants with a waiting list of 100 will be accepted through the lottery in 1984.

An additional method to gain entry is called Ironman Qualifiers (IQ's). Race officials have selected various triathlons throughout the country which allow automatic acceptance into Ironman for the overall male and female winners and for some of the age group winners. In addition to all the Bud Light USTS races, 25 other triathlons were selected as IQ's for the 1984 race.

Furthermore, a check payable to Ironman for $100, which is refunded if you are denied acceptance, is another aspect of the required paperwork. Although this may seem high, the awards, dinners, and race day foods for each contestant easily match the value of the entry fee.

Assuming you are accepted, your next step should be to confirm condominium and plane reservations. Horror stories flow freely about past contestants who arrived in Oahu but couldn't get an interisland flight to the Kona coast on the "Big Island" where the race is held. Approximately 4,000 people will compete for housing in an area which normally serves a small tourist and sport fishermen population.

Reservations need to be made on the basis of your arrival and departure dates. I personally feel you should allow a liberal lead time for course and environmental familiarization. My own arrival was 3 weeks prior to the race date, giving me 2 weeks of intense-accelerated training as well as a week to taper. In retrospect, I am grateful for all 21 days but, frankly, would not have wanted any more. Departure dates are usually made for the Monday following Saturday's race. The awards banquet, a sterling event, is held on Sunday evening; and Monday morning is valuable, usually spent crating up your bike and relearning how to walk.

Your arrival on the Big Island will probably be at the Keahole Airport on the Kona coast. As you depart the plane, you will formulate at least two false impressions. First, you will see what you'd expect to see in Hawaii—palm trees. Rest assured, they are imports and may be the last ones you see until you board for home! Except for a few areas between the town of Kailua and the bike finish/run start area, the course looks like a plate of uncut brownies.

You will note the second false impression when you participate in the "parade of the stars" at the baggage pick-up area. The stars, of course, are the triathletes who have preceded your arrival. They have come to pick up other members of their "club," and you are now the spectator. I vividly remember this intimidating experience because it left me feeling less than competitive. Ironically, I never once saw any of the "stars" again—not in training, not in competition, and not as award recipients! I suspect, as in all sports, there is a social element that also attracts many to the Ironman. Just being there is satisfying enough for many.

Many times I saw the same people in deep conversation when I entered the water for an hour's workout and still in deep conversation when I returned. Furthermore, be confident that on any day, at any time, the trip to Hawi (the bicycle turn-around point) will be very lonely. So don't let the "parade of stars" discourage you in any way. How you look, who you know, and what you say are poor predictors of how you'll finish!

The Ironman Course

Swim Course

Once you've settled into your new abode, you will no doubt want that first taste of salt water. If you have any fears of the swim course—tides, living creatures, swells, and so on—put them to rest for the Ironman swim course is nothing short of wonderful! The water temperature is perfect (even in the early morning); the salty taste is easily tolerated; waves, swells, and currents are hardly noticeable, and the sea life poses no danger to swimmers. About all you will need to be concerned with here is a population of sea urchins that cling to the rocks as you wade out to chest-deep water at the swim courses entrance. Stepping on these seemingly harmless creatures could cut your foot, hardly the threat anticipated. Once you're into the swim, prepare yourself for a real Polynesian treat. Swimming in the the crystal-clear water is like swimming in a giant aquarium—schools of beautifully colored fish peacefully swim by as if you were one of them. Remains of shipwrecks still litter the ocean's bottom. You can see the ocean's bottom at all places, even those as much as 90 feet deep. During my stay in Kona, I swam over 25 miles in those waters and never once was confronted with a life-threatening experience. Contestants and officials alike strongly recommend that you wear an orange-colored swim cap and not swim alone. This is good advice but seldom heeded. Unless you have some kind of "blood" relationship with another competitor, don't expect to stay partnered up very long.

The swim course takes on a rectangular shape on the day of competition. A few days before the race, officials mark the course every .2 miles with large, orange buoys. In training, however, very little directs your swimming.

From the vantage point of the sandy beach where the breaker wall meets Kailua Pier, you will swim parallel with both the pier and the shoreline on your left. The course direction is approximately straight toward the point where the sloping hillside meets the water. When on course, you will most often be about 100 yards from shore.

Until the orange buoys are in place, only two reliable landmarks offer you accurate distances. The first is the "ski jump" structure on the Hilton Hotel. When directly in line with this architecture, you have just completed 0.7 miles. The other distance marker is the turn-around buoy that race officials put out approximately 1 month before the race. What you look for is two or three air-filled plastic jugs tied together, floating 1.2 miles onto the course. Good luck finding this marker! Unless by happenstance you come upon it, you will never find it. Several swells will block your view and most likely separate you from the plastic bottles at all times.

Fortunately, sighting for the return swim is considerably easier. The King Kamehameha Hotel is a good target. The hotel is actually two buildings, both

Figure 10.1 The Ironman swim course.

six or seven stories high. Sight for the northernmost structure and you will head directly to the Kailua Pier. Most swimmers, when training, keep the pier on their left and return to the small beach area from where they entered the water. The actual race, however, finishes at the boat landing on the north side of the pier. It is a good idea to avoid this area in training, but please try swimming to the boat landing once or twice before race day. Figure 10.1 illustrates the Ironman swim course.

What time of day you swim is also worth considering. Most triathletes gather at the pier between 7 and 9 a.m.—the best time of finding someone to swim with. I believe the early morning swim time is best for the triathletes for several reasons. First, the actual swim phase of the race begins at 7 a.m., so you might as well give your body the needed exposure. Second, boat traffic picks up around 8:30 a.m. The pier serves as a loading/unloading site for several tourist boats; it is also the distribution center for several sport fishing rigs. For the most part, the skippers are extremely aware and cautious of the seasonal swimming population, so I am not suggesting that danger is eminent when the boat population picks up. Possibly the worst time to swim is when the sport fishing boats return to the pier to register the day's catch. This begins around 3:30 in the afternoon and can continue until supper time.

Bicycle Course

Coming from the Midwest where potholes are custom-built to receive 700 C diameter wheels, I expected to find similar conditions on Kona's roads. But to my pleasant surprise, I found the roads to be silky smooth, adequately wide, and lightly traveled. Since lava rock is synonymous with the Big Island, it's understandable that the roads would be made of the same. Although the road seems smooth, it is actually quite coarse. To paper-thin racing tires, this surface becomes particularly abrasive. I remember getting two flats on the way to Hawi one morning, only to get a third on the way back. The final flat occurred at about 30 mph which made the frustration slightly exciting, to say the least.

There are lessons to be learned: Carry at least two spares on all rides, both in training and in competition; make sure your tires have plenty of tread and/or are well-seasoned; and finally, consider not using repaired tubulars on the course. The black road surface heats up considerably as the day progresses and can raise tire pressure by at least 10 psi, making restitched casings extra vulnerable.

Deal with your gearing needs prior to arrival on Polynesian Rock. In chapter 6, I suggested that Ironman is a course of extremes: Certain parts are downhill with tremendous tail winds, but other areas are just the opposite. Be prepared to go as slow as 7 mph, and as fast as 40+ mph. The only hill worth mentioning is at around mile 110 when you are in no mood to face (much less attack) hills. I took it in a 42/22 combination but could have used a little extra gearing if I'd had it.

We shall now consider the course proper. Starting from Kailua Pier, the swim to bike transition area, the course begins with a fairly respectable quarter-mile

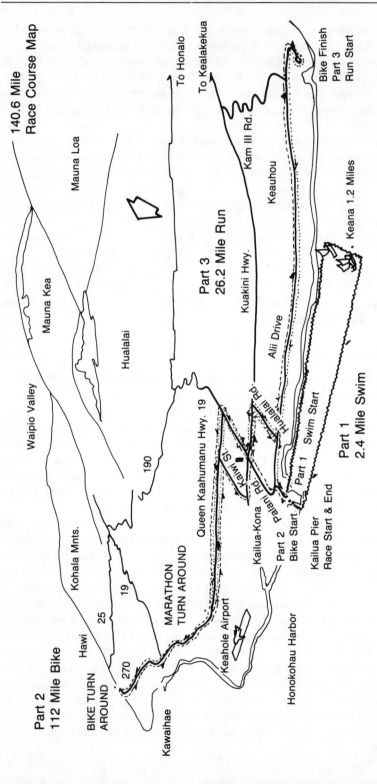

Figure 10.2 The Ironman bike and run course. Taken from the Official Race Guide of the 1983 Ironman Triathlon World Championship, (p. 69). Reprinted with permission.

ascent before heading north onto the Queen Kaahumanu (Queen's) Highway. For the next 30 miles, you head north through some very underwhelming country. If it weren't for some palm tree transplants marking the entrance to Mauna Lani at around Mile 25, you would think you were on the moon!

Most of the road is flat with intermittent rolling hills along the first 30 miles. In the first 12 miles, expect mild crosswinds from the southeast, which generally push you along. At Mile 8 you pass the airport, and at Mile 12 you pass a resort oasis. I call this an oasis because the management sets out a cooler of ice water each morning for thirsty bikers. Knowing that oasis water is waiting, the return trip is much more tolerable. Figure 10.2 illustrates the bike course, including the changing wind directions.

Somewhere between Mile 15 and Mile 20 you can expect the winds to confront you head on. The wind velocity varies tremendously, but seldom do you confront the next 10 to 15 miles without some unmentionables stemming from your vocabulary. My first ride out to Hawi was particularly depressing because I had underestimated the seriousness of these winds. What motivated me to press on was knowing how easy the return trip would be with the winds to my back. You have probably heard of the yin and yang of cycling: For every uphill there is a downhill, for every head wind there is a tail wind. Indeed, the course had a few double yangs! On the return ride the winds shifted, and I had the same exhausting experience on the return trip. I was so tired that I remember walking my bike a few blocks just for a mental break.

At about Mile 32, you drop into Kawaihae, a quiet town blending well into the desolate countryside. At the base of the hill you pass a tavern (the turn-around point for many triathletes), and then prepare to branch north again for Hawi. A gas station where the road bends will be your last water stop before the final lonely grind to the turn-around point, another 18 miles away.

The stretch from Kawaihae to Hawi takes you up about 500 feet, just enough to get the full effect of the relentless trade winds. The worst stretch tends to be the last 7 or 8 miles before the turn-around point, but you may confront vicious head winds for an hour or more along this stretch.

The actual turn-around point is positioned on the hilltop overlooking the four or five stores making up the downtown area of Hawi. Be on the lookout for what appears to be a feedstore on your left; actually, it is a movie theater, and billboards to that effect can be seen if you know what to look for.

If your water supply is low, consider refilling, but realize that the 18-mile return trip to Kawaihae goes very quickly. This return trip will easily register speeds over 35 mph, so maintain caution especially as you jet over several cattle-crossing grates. These grates are not dangerous if you maintain a straight ride, rise off the seat a little, and hold on.

Upon returning to Kawaihae, you must fill all water bottles because you will most likely confront more head winds before the next water stop 18 miles away. From Kawaihae you confront a relatively steep ascent before heading south once again on the Queen K Highway. If luck is on your side, the return trip will include either tail winds or crosswinds; otherwise, you could be pedaling the remaining 30 miles with great difficulty. I have made this return stretch in less than 1 hour but have also been on it for over 2 hours. Most of the time you can expect the first half of this southerly stretch to be tail winds, and the last half to be either crosswinds or mild (15 mph) head winds.

Upon returning to Kailua-Kona, you will have registered 105 of the 112-mile course. What remains is the mile stretch through town onto Alii Drive, and the 6-mile push along the coast to the Kona Surf Hotel. This stretch to the hotel is flat with calm winds for the first 4 miles but laden with heavy traffic. Most of the resort hotels and area beaches reside along this stretch of road. The narrow road then begins a series of hills that within a mile's distance crescendoes to at least 500 feet above the coast. Once at the top, be prepared to turn into the Kona Surf Hotel on a road which drops very quickly, giving you speeds in excess of 35 mph.

Run Course

In training you will probably begin your runs from the Kailua-Kona area and either head north toward the airport or south to the Kona Surf Hotel. But because the actual race begins at the Kona Surf, the run course as you would run it in competition is as follows: From the Kona Surf Hotel, the first few steps take you to the base of a very steep hill. Not only is it steep, but it is long. Within a half to three-quarters of a mile, you climb back up to 500 feet. Most of the ascent happens within the first quarter mile—just what you need after 112 miles of cycling!

Once on top, however, your trip into Kailua-Kona is very relaxing and takes you through some beautiful countryside. The ocean tends to remain at your side with more typical Hawaiian foliage shading much of your course. About 2 miles into the course, you have the opportunity to refill the water bottle you are carrying. Hidden in a residential hedge on the ocean side of the road is a drinking fountain for public use. This fountain is about the only water available between Kailua and the Kona Surf Hotel, so be sure to locate it early in your training.

When you get into Kailua, the course winds through town up a steep ascent on Palani Road to the Queen K Highway where the bike phase began. If you think the Queen K is desolate on a bicycle, try it running! Without the breeze created from biking, the runner has to contend with heat, traffic, and repressive scenery—and all with little opportunity to cool off. The course continues past the airport for another 1.5 to 2 miles to its turn-around point. There is no landmark suggesting this location, so you will need to estimate, using the airport as a landmark. The return trip is once again into town on the Queen K and takes you through town, down onto Alii Drive, and finishes at the pier where it all began. Figure 10.2 provides you with an overview of the run course.

If you reside in Kailua (which most do), you will probably begin and finish your run workouts in town. From town to the Kona Surf Hotel and back, the distance is about 14 miles with two water stops—at the hotel and in the hedge. When you run out toward the airport, remember that this 8-mile stretch between town and the airport is completely void of water, so you must carry your own. What I did was to freeze a full water bottle and tucked it in a sock before leaving. The sock served as insulation, protecting my hand from the frozen bottle. Between town and the airport, I would sip away on the melting ice. By the time I got to the airport, the bottle was empty, but I would continue to the turn-around point. Once back to the airport entrance, I would make a half-mile detour to refill my bottle at one of the airport drinking fountains. With 8 miles to go, I could usually make the return trip without getting excessively dehydrated. Estimating that this route is slightly under 20 miles, I always rewarded myself with a giant snow cone from the Saved Ice Co., a location which becomes the temporary headquarters for all triathletes.

The Ironman Race

Prerace Activities

Ironman activities officially begin with equipment check-in on the Wednesday and Thursday immediately preceding Saturday's race. At that time you bag up all running and cycling gear, and receive your tickets to the carbo-loading party and awards banquet, plus your first bag of souvenirs. Thursday evening is the carbo-loading party, which is a much better idea than having it the night before as most races do. On Friday, you must take your bike through the safety check at which time officials corral your bike in its reserved place. If you've placed in the top 100 the year before, you receive the prime spots—right in front of the changing tents. The rest of the numbers are awarded alphabetically. This system reminded me of grade school days, where as a "T", I routinely found myself in the last row in nearly the last seat. For me, No. 999 was clear down at the pier's end. Officials allow you access to your bicycle the morning of the race to pump up tires, load water bottles, and so forth. Figure l0.3 represents the facility layout of Kailu Pier the morning of the race.

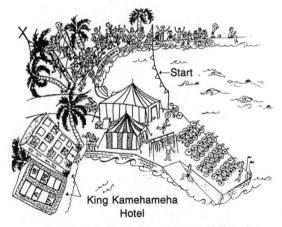

Figure 10.3 Race day setting on Kailua pier.

With all your equipment checked in except for the swim gear, you now have nothing more to do than to allow your mind to take you through periods of doubt, fear, tension, and anger. For me, the 10½ hours before the race were much worse than the 10½ hours during the race. Even after 7 months of intense training, 1,000 miles of training on Hawaii roads, 25 miles of Hawaii ocean training, $5,000 of fund-raising efforts, and hundreds of supporters holding me up in prayer, I would still have preferred to go home instead of going for it! Maybe it was just all the prerace hype, maybe it was the sheer reality that what I had come for was finally here; whatever it was—I wanted out!

The night before the race was hardly what you would call a "safe and restful sleep." Frankly, I'm surprised the mattress didn't wear out from all the tossing and turning. Starting at 5 a.m., contestants were allowed to be numbered on the shoulders and thighs at the pier area. After such a disappointing night's rest, I decided to saunter down to the pier and was very relieved to see that hundreds of other contestants were no doubt experiencing the same restlessness. Even in the pitch black early morning hour, most of the pier area was filled with spectators willing to sacrifice sleep for the best seats. After getting numbered, I returned to the condo feeling much better about my sleepless condition.

I had a light breakfast with my family; then we all walked to the start area. I will never forget that quarter-mile walk. I felt as if I were walking toward a noose sponsored by a lynch mob! Reflecting back, it must have been all the fanfare that was so intimidating: Thousands of people, helicopters, and planes everywhere, camera crews on scaffolding, in boats, up on cherry-picker hoists; announcers blaring away—what a psyche out!

At about 6:50, swimmers started placing themselves for the start of the swim. This area is rather opened up, providing adequate space for all; but I found it interesting as to how the contestants had seeded themselves. The best swimmers hovered in deep water just under the string of overhead triangular flags which marked the start. I estimated that 100 to 200 swimmers took positions in front. To my surprise, almost everyone else was crowded against the breaker wall as far back from the start as one could get! I was wise enough to stay clear of the torpedo-like swimmers, but on the other hand, certainly was more interested in a better starting position than the wall. So I paddled out to shoulder-deep water, found a rock free of sea urchins, and contentedly awaited the countdown.

The Race

The start of the race is well-known for its spectacle of arms and foam, but it will soon be as well-known for its blatant false start. With 10 seconds to go before the start, everyone was well on their way. People say that a cannon starts the race, but it's doubtful whether any contestant ever heard it. Having had a clean start, I was getting uninterrupted strokes for the first few minutes. But it wasn't long before swimmers better than I started up my heels and crowded me on both sides. As expected, arms were tied up in others' arms and feet. Most of the swim remained crowded, and efforts to draft and go straight failed miserably. Despite these inconveniences, the swim went as expected, and I finished in 1:18, 8 minutes off prediction, right in the middle of the competition. Most importantly, I had survived the swim, and the race was finally underway. Once on the boat ramp, officials help you get your footing. You then remove the swim I.D. tag and run under a series of overhead hoses supplying the swimmers with fresh water for drinking and for rinsing off. Next, you are handed your bag of cycling gear and whisked into the changing tent. After a quick change, contestants load up with food and are escorted to the bicycle. Reflecting on this phase of the race, I am grateful that I got onto the road without an accident, for this area of the race is mass confusion, enhanced by the thousands of spectators peering on the course for that split-second glimpse of their personal favorite. My wife, Nancy, was both excited and relieved to see me finally out of the water for good and onto my stronger events.

On the Queen K Highway, the race finally settled down. The course is closed to everyone except for Ironmen and the press, so congestion was finally behind us. Although some concerns were eliminated, new ones were created. During much of my training rides, I had nothing to do but stare blankly down at the highway or watch my pumping knees. This habit cost me two near crashes as I abruptly came up on slower competitors.

Another new problem associated with the race is the series of aid stations located every 5 miles on the bike course. These desert oases represent the epitome of organization by the station volunteers, but the exact opposite by the contestants. I quickly learned to stay clear of bikers ahead because their actions were totally unpredictable. A typical aid station was 100+ yards long with probably 50 volunteers manning each one. As you ride by, you drop off your used water bottles and then make a menu selection, cafeteria-style. Whenever I signaled to a volunteer who had what I wanted, he or she would dash off in the direction of travel, looking straight ahead with the food choice held out onto the road. This system left no guessing whether my hand would coordinate with the volunteer's and vice versa. Each station provided the competitors with orange sections, bananas, chocolate chip cookies, guava jam sandwiches, cold sponges, and water bottles full of water and Gatorade. I normally carried a bottle of water, one of Gatorade, as many cookies as I could get, and a couple of bananas.

On the way out, the winds were worse than any of my 900+ training miles. Winds with tremendous velocity came up earlier in the ride. At least 2 hours of the ride out was at speeds less than 10 mph! For the competition who hadn't acclimated to these winds by means of on-location training rides, this experience must have been demoralizing. Because I continued passing people on a regular basis, my spirits remained high. At Hawi, you actually turn off the highway and are routed through a checkpoint/aid station before being directed back onto the highway. The turn-around point is a welcome sight, as we all were anticipating the tremendous tail winds and overall downhill advantages. But what I didn't anticipate was the trouble other contestants were having trying to stay in their own lane. At 40+ mph, I was confronted with others barely moving right in my path: I was petrified. Apart from this unwelcomed thrill of playing "dodge bike," the return trip to Kailua went as planned. Fortunately, I was spared from being a victim of the "tack attack"—a deviant scheme where someone had thrown carpet tacks onto the highway.

Once in Kailua, we all got another split-second glimpse of family and friends before making the final push to the Kona Surf Hotel. For many, the winds had taken its toll, and people were now walking bicycles up those final hills which climax the bike phase of Ironman. The fast descent into the hotel was shared by runners making their way up. Although not dangerous, it was an area in which to use caution.

The bike ride finishes at the lower level of the hotel where volunteers whisk your machine away and escort you into the hotel. A large clock notes the contestants' progress, but doubtless anyone really cared. I was pleased to find I had moved up over 300 places to 105th at the end of the ride.

Once inside the hotel, a large room was sectioned off for changing purposes. There, nurses helped you with the change while they observe you for signs of excessive fatigue or dehydration. Portable toilets line the hotel and serve as a helpful way to start the run. The base of the steep ascent offers you the first of 26 aid stations for runners. Every mile the volunteers waited to serve you the food and drink described previously, plus cups of coke and ice. Bikers still on the course were not offered food at the runners' aid stations, so I felt the run phase was very safe and trouble-free.

Back through Kailua (with one last glimpse of family and friends), we all settled in for the long tiring run. My biggest concern with the run was dehydration. At each aid station I took a cup of ice water, immediately sipped off the top third, and folded over the top to seal the valuable liquid. I carried the cup like a lunch bucket and slowly sipped away until the next aid station appeared, where I'd start the cycle all over again. For most of the run, I ate nothing solid and drank only ice water. My major concern was fluid replacement, so in no way did I want to slow the fluid absorption rate by consuming sugar-based foods or liquids. This worked for the first 18 miles, but then I began to "hit the wall." For the next two aid stations, I drank a full cup of Coke and the symptoms disappeared. Then for the remainder of the run, I went back to consuming water only. With 2 miles to go, leg cramps started to set in but never increased to a disabling intensity.

Once back in town, the thrill of knowing that I was going to finish better than 50 places over prediction carried me down Alii Drive feeling—uh, well, let your own imagination take over from here! At the finish, you are donned a finisher's lei by the race director and receive another bag of finisher's souvenirs. Expect a medical bodyguard to follow you around until you can convince this person you're not going to phase out. Whenever you are ready, a battalion of massage therapists are waiting. My rubdown actually left me very stiff, and I regret not having walked around more beforehand.

Reflecting back on my Ironman experience, the most impressive aspect of the on-site training phase was the community interest and support. What impressed me most about the race was the organization and the 3,000+ volunteers. These people do a wonderful job, more than I am capable of articulating. To see these volunteers in action is as impressive as watching the athletes themselves. They are committed, excited, and highly trained. Some of the aid station teams were practicing weekly to get in shape for their Ironman—support-style.

Chapter 11

Triathlon Injuries and Injury Prevention

Most of the information on injuries to triathletes is rather optimistic. Despite the long, arduous training hours required of the sport, the dispersion of work over three different events suggests an opportunity for some areas of the body to rest and recover while others are being stressed. In her book, *Triathlon: A Triple Fitness Sport,* Sally Edwards (1983) states:

> A triathlete can use the diversity of the triple-event sport to create rest opportunities without much letup in the work load. Remember the specificity commandment: swimming is a rest for the legs; biking, a free ride for the swimming muscles. Even running and biking, though using many of the same leg muscles, are different enough for each to serve as a resting activity for the other.

Kranzley (1983) claims that overuse injuries can be avoided, and training time lost from injuries that do occur can be kept to a minimum by triple training. Another vote in favor of injury prevention for triathletes is the fact that triathlons are performed at submaximal levels. The race does not demand an all out performance, sprint strategies, and the like. Triathlons require a calculated distribution of effort based on an individual's strengths and weaknesses.

This could well be a key benefit because most injuries among conditioned athletes occur at high levels of intensity. Runners pull the hamstring muscle in attempts to force their stride, cyclists come up lame in the finish line sprint, and swimmers strain their shoulders in their attempts to stave off competitors.

Efforts to address triathlon-related injuries have mainly come from an examination of the typical injuries associated with swimming, cycling, and running as separate events. When injuries are viewed in this way, injury patterns are formed which can caution triathletes. What are some of these troublesome sites?

Sport-Specific Injuries

Swimming Injuries

Richardson (1980) claims that shoulder pain is the most common orthopedic problem among competitive swimmers, having been reported to be 40 to 60% in this population (Dominguez, 1980). Swimmer's shoulder represents a pain located at the front of the shoulder. According to Dominguez (1979), this pain is the result of restricted blood flow to the tendons of the shoulder causing the tendons to become swollen and tender. This swelling create pressure on the shoulder joint, resulting in pain. Constant breathing to one side and the use of hand paddles increase the likelihood of swimmer's shoulder (Brunet, 1982). About the only other swimming injury associated with the front crawl stroke is a form of tendinitis in the ankle area caused from pointing the toes in the flutter kick (Roy & Irvin, 1983).

Cycling Injuries

Crashes are the most common source of injury among cyclists. Competitive cyclists crash because of tire blowouts or from colliding into other cyclists (Edwards, 1983). Recreational cyclists, on the other hand, crash because of sandy road surfaces while turning or going downhill (Davis, Litman, Crenshaw, & Mueller, 1980). Although crash-related injuries among competitive cyclists are rather rare, fractured clavicles and abrasions to the hip, elbow, and knee are the more common occurrences. In a study by Bohlmann (1981), preventive measures include keeping the bicycle in top mechanical condition, wearing strong, durable clothing and a helmet, and knowing how to fall.

When examining cycling injuries apart from crashes, the knees, hands, and buttocks become the more common injury sites. According to Gaston (1979), the knees are susceptible to several injuries in cycling: chondromalacia (pain behind the knee cap), sprains, strains, and to a lesser extent, bursitis. Gaston cites the cause of knee pain as mainly from improper saddle height and from pushing too hard in higher gears. Powell (1982) suggests that improper saddle height can also lead to other discomforts ranging from leg and hip pain to soreness, chafing, and irritation of the crotch.

Finally, a problem often reported among long-distance cyclists is ulnar neuropathy, a numbness, weakness, and loss of coordination in one or both hands (Burke, 1981). Burke suggests several corrective measures which include using well padded bicycling gloves, padded handlebars, correct frame size, correct distance from seat to stem, and frequent changing of hand positions on the handlebars. Other problem areas among competitive cyclists include the neck, shoulders, lower back, and thigh (Bohlmann, 1981).

Running Injuries

That running is plagued with injuries is not surprising. Running involves a series of "hops" that require a single leg to support and to absorb a tremendous impact in repeated fashion. Given a stride length of 3 feet, 880 cycles would be required for the legs to cover 1 mile. If you run 40 miles per week, each leg would be required to absorb the impact of your entire body 35,200 times weekly or 1,830,400 times per year!

In 1977, *Runner's World* magazine surveyed the problem of running-related injuries (Henderson, 1977). The survey's results indicated that 2 out of 3 runners were afflicted by injuries each year. The area of injury reported was almost always from the hip down with the knee taking the highest percentage of injuries. Table 11.1 lists the incidence of running injuries from the *Runner's World* survey. Multiple injuries to the same runner was given as the reason why the total percentage was greater than 100%.

Once the area of injury is localized, the diagnosis is often extremely complex. In a retrospective survey of the clinical records of 1,650 patients seeking treatment for running injuries, Clement and others (1981) identified 19 different injuries to the knee, 13 to the lower leg, and 22 different diagnoses to the foot. Gaining an understanding of the injuries in these three areas alone requires such "high tech" terminology and troubleshooting efforts that orthopedics themselves cannot agree on a diagnosis, let alone explain it to the lay public.

Regardless how you label running injuries, the most common problem to the knee is chondromalacia. Shinsplints plague the lower leg, and plantar fasciitis ranks number one in the foot (Brody, 1980; Krissoff & Ferris, 1979; Scranton & Stanitski, 1978). All three of these terms are generalizations of some very specific diagnosis.

Chondromalacia, for instance, is a term used to describe any pain located in the patellar femoral region. What this term really describes is a softening of the undersurface of the patella (kneecap). Normally the patella runs smoothly in its

TABLE 11.1   Incidence of Running Injuries

Anatomical Site	Incidence
Knee	25%
Achilles tendon	18%
Shin	15%
Ankle	11%
Heel	10%
Arch	8%
Calf	7%
Hip	7%
Hamstrings	6%
Forefoot	6%

Note: From "First aid for the injured" by J. Henderson. 1977, *Runner's World,* **12**, 32-37. Reprinted with permission from *Runner's World.*

groves on the femur (thighbone). However, stresses may cause the patella to deviate from the normal groove, resulting in the softening and in the incorrect tracking of patella. Some of the stresses causing chondromalacia include knock-knees, bowlegs, and flat feet.

Subotnick (1977) generalizes about knee problems in runners and suggests improper foot pronation and thigh alignment as the leading causes. Subotnick suggests that knee pain can be avoided by strengthening the muscles that stabilize the knee, namely the quadriceps and hamstrings.

Shinsplints is actually a catchall term describing any pain between the ankle and knee. The term can be used to describe stress fractures, tendinitis, and/or periostitis of the tibia and fibula bones of the lower leg.

According to Roy and Irvin (1983), the cause of shinsplints is abnormal foot pronation, requiring other muscles of the foot to provide the stabilization. Since these muscles are not designed to provide this support, microtearing results at the muscle's attachment sites. Ice, massage, rest, and antiinflammatory medication are generally needed for cure.

Achilles peritendinitis is a tearing and inflammation affecting the largest tendon in the body and is almost always the result of overtraining or of using worn-out running shoes. Treatment is the same as for the stress fracture, along with the need to purchase shoes with adequate cushion in the heel strike area.

The foot also suffers from injury when running and ranks third in anatomical sites for running injuries. The most common foot injury according to Clement (1981) and Brody (1980) is plantar fasciitis, commonly called the "heel spur syndrome." Similar to achilles tendinitis, this problem is an overuse injury that involves an inflammatory reaction on the undersurface of the heel bone called the calcaneus. Heel pads, plastic heel cups, rest, and ice are often the first line of therapy. Antiinflammatory drugs and rest are the more drastic treatments.

The constant pounding that running requires sets up a chain reaction in the joints and muscles felt most in the foot, lower leg, and knee. Although the trauma is inevitable, injury does not necessarily have to be the outcome. Proper footwear, good running form, and the ability to maintain proper body weight are the necessary ingredients that must be combined with a sensible training schedule in order to experience injury free-running.

Triathlon-Related Injuries

As you study the injuries in all sports required of the triathlon, you will conclude that the knee is a common problem area. Sally Edwards (1983) also saw this portion of anatomy as a trouble spot and labeled it as the "triathlete-knee syndrome" which she describes as follows:

> Many triathletes complain about triathlete knee. The knee is the most infamous joint in sports because it is subject to particular injury. Its construction as both a hinge joint and a lever joint requires that it be both mobile and stable.

These are contradictory demands. The triathlete-knee syndrome is caused by the contrasting action on the knee in the two leg-propelled sports. When the triathlete cycles, the knee joint is pulled apart and stretched. When the triathlete runs, the knee joint is slammed together and tightened. The opposing actions can be wrenching. Swimming does not seem to hurt the knees and may even be therapeutic.

Apart from the speculations made by Edwards and Kranzley, the research lacks any investigative efforts into the injury patterns of triathletes. Does the triathlete get injured? If so, what are the injury patterns, and are they similar to those realized in the sports that separately make up the triathlon? These were some of the questions that motivated researcher Sanford Bates and me to scientifically investigate the problem of athletic injuries in triathletes (Bates & Town, 1985). We recently surveyed all applicants to the 1982 Menomonie (Wisconsin) Tin Man Triathlon and the October 1982 Ironman Triathlon World Championship in Hawaii in efforts to resolve this injury question. Menomonie's Tin Man race was chosen because of its intermediate distances (1mi swim, 55mi bike and 12.4mi run) and its rugged environmental conditions. The course was extremely hilly and hot. Ironman was an obvious choice because of the seriousness of its competitors, and its challenging distances and environmental conditions.

For Menomonie, 330 surveys were sent and 176 of the applicants responded, giving us a return of 53.3%. For the Ironman, 904 surveys were sent and 318 of the contestants submitted data, representing a return of 35.2%. Table 11.2

TABLE 11.2   Physical Characteristics of Triathletes

	Tinman		Ironman	
	Males	Females	Males	Females
Number of subjects	151	17	276	35
Average age (yrs.)	33.7	31.0	33.9	32.9
Height (in.)	70.4	66.0	70.2	65.5
Weight	159.9	127.1	160.2	125.4
Number of triathlons competed	4.9	3.4	7.2	8.5
Hours/week swim training	2.7	3.5	4.5	4.7
Hours/week bike training	8.5	10.1	11.7	13.9
Hours/week run training	5.5	6.2	7.3	7.9
Miles/week swim training	4.0	5.0	6.8	7.0
Miles/week bike training	124.9	126.4	189.0	206.2
Miles/week run training	35.9	34.6	47.4	45.7

TABLE 11.3   Physical Characteristics of Elite Cyclists and Distance Runners

Group	Number	Hgt	Wgt	Reference
Male Triathletes	427	70.3	160.0	Bates & Town, 1984
Female Triathletes	52	65.7	126.0	Bates & Town, 1984
Elite Distance Runners	14	70.4	140.8	Costill et al., 1976
Men's National Cycling Team	12	71.0	156.1	Burke, 1980
Category I Men Cyclists	8	71.1	151.2	Burke, 1980
Women's National Team	7	66.0	135.1	Burke, 1980
1968 Men's World Cycling Championships	40	68.9	154.3	Vank, 1973

describes the physical characteristics and training profiles of the subjects responding to the surveys.

Table 11.3 compares the physical characteristics of our triathlete population to elite swimming, cycling, and running competitors. It is interesting to note that male triathletes are shorter than runners, as tall as cyclists, but heavier than both cyclists and runners. Data on women athletes is rather limited with small sample sizes, making it difficult to draw any conclusions.

When asked to rate their strengths in the three events, 25.1% of the male respondents ranked swimming as their best event, 30% thought cycling was their best, and 44.9% rated running as number one. Women responded about the same as men in ranking swimming number one (26%), but interestingly enough, ranked cycling (38%) slightly higher than running (34.4%) as the strongest event.

To get at the question of injuries, we first classified each response into 1 of 5 different categories:

Category I: Applied but did not compete

Category II: Trained and competed without injury

Category III: Injured while training only, but still competed

Category IV: Injured in competition, but not in training

Category V: Experienced injury in both training and in competition

The number of injuries under each category is listed for the two races surveyed in Table 11.4.

In Category I, we were puzzled why such a low percentage of the Ironman applicants who were accepted did not compete. This data is deceiving because we knew that 54 fewer contestants arrived at the start of Ironman than were accepted. In reality, only 4 of those 54 applicants responded to our survey. Lifestyle

TABLE 11.4   Classification of Triathlete's Injury Categories

Category	Tinman	Ironman
I	26(14.8%)	4(1.3%)
II	104(59.1%)	150(47.2%)
III	34(19.3%)	119(37.4%)
IV	7(4%)	16(5.0%)
V	5(2.8%)	29(9.1%)

changes, finances, inadequate time to train, and serious injuries were the main reasons why those who were accepted did not compete. In the Tinman data, 10 out of 26 reported injuries as the reason for not competing: 3 were localized in the knee, 2 in the upper leg, 2 in the lower back, 1 in the lower leg, 1 in the shoulder, and 1 in the arm.

In Category II, the greatest number of competitors trained and competed injury-free. The percentage of Ironman competitors in this category was considerably fewer than those who trained and competed injury-free in the Tinman competition. This data was believed to be indicative of the added training time that Ironman competitors committed over and above those competitors in Tinman. The Tinman competitors averaged 16.7 hours/week in training, whereas Ironman competitors averaged 23.4 hours/week. Women committed 3 additional training hours over the men in both races.

Category III considered all competitors who were injured in training but were either able to recover in time to compete, or the injury was not severe enough to prevent the athlete from competing. Almost twice the percentage of Ironmen as did Tinman competitors fell into this category. For the Ironman competitors, the knee accounted for 51% of the training injuries, the lower leg for 27.9%, and the ankle for 26.7% of the injuries. In Tinman, the knee had the most injuries (33.3%) with the lower leg (27.3%) and the ankle (24%) second and third highest, respectively.

Race day injuries, classified as Category IV, were relatively few. Those who were injured both in training and competition, Category V, were also relatively few in Tinman, but in Ironman a large portion of this group had knee injuries. Table 11.5 lists the injuries by category and by training event in which the injury occurred.

Swimming injuries represented 10 to 11% of all injuries incurred in both races. Although the shoulder was the anatomical site with the most injuries, it is considerably less than the shoulder injury rate reported by Richardson (1980) on competitive swimmers, and certainly not enough of a problem to be listed as a common injury to triathletes as suggested by Edwards (1983). A bigger problem than swimmer's shoulder in our survey was foot abrasions from stepping on sharp objects upon entering and leaving the water.

Probably the large discrepancy between shoulder injuries in triathletes and that of competitive swimmers is due to the lesser intensity and frequency that triathletes swim. Competitive swimmers often swim twice daily with very demanding high-intensity workouts. The triathletes in our study swam an average of 4 hours per week.

Table 11.5   Triathlon Injuries Classified by Training Event and Category

Event	Anatomical Site	Tinman					Ironman				
				Category					Category		
		I	III	IV	V	Total	I	III	IV	V	Total
Swim	Foot		1	1		2		3	1	2	5
	Ankle		1			1		1			1
	Lower leg							4	1		5
	Knee		1			1	1	1		1	3
	Upper leg								1		1
	Hip								1		1
	Lower back	1				1		1		2	3
	Shoulder	1	2			3		6		1	7
	Other		1			1					
	Total	2	6	1		9	1	15	4	6	26
Bike	Foot		1	1		2		2		2	4
	Ankle		1			1		3	2	3	8
	Lower leg							4	1	3	8
	Knee		2	1	2	5		22	3	19	44
	Upper leg	1		1		2		2	4	2	8
	Hip		2		1	3		6	3	1	10
	Lower back	1			1	2		4		5	9
	Shoulder	1	1			2.		8	2	2	12
	Other		1			1		1			1
	Total	3	8	3	4	18	0	52	17	35	104

Table 11.5   cont.

Run	Foot		4	1	3	8		17	2	7	24
	Ankle		6			6		19		6	15
	Lower leg	1	9		3	13		16		8	24
	Knee	2	7	3		12	1	21		15	37
	Upper leg	1	2	2		5		4			4
	Hip		2			2		8		1	9
	Lower back	2	3			5		3		1	4
	Shoulder										
	Other										
	Total	6	33	6	6	51	1	86	2	38	127
	Combined totals					78					257

Bicycling injuries accounted for 23.1% and 40.2% of the total injuries in the Tinman and Ironman competitors, respectively. The Ironman count includes a high number of injuries from crashes—27 injuries in all. Subtracting these crash-related injuries from the total cycling injury count, the ratio drops to 33%.

Knee injury from cycling was the greatest source of injury in the entire survey, accounting for 17% of all Ironman injuries. Five of the knee injuries were crash-related, and even when these were removed from the total, the knee from cycling was still the most injured site of the triathletes surveyed. Respondents offered 17 different knee injuries as diagnoses which included tendons, ligaments, patella, and cartilage problems. No other anatomical site suffered greatly from cycle training and competition.

Running-related injuries represented approximately two-thirds of all injuries in the Tinman competitors and almost half of the Ironman injuries. As noted in Table 11.5, a heavy incidence of Ironman running injuries were experienced in the knee (37), ankle (25), lower leg (24) and foot (24). In the Tinman race, the ankle received the most running-related injuries at 13, followed closely by 12 injuries to the knee.

Eighteen different knee injury diagnoses were reported; these included muscle pulls and strains, ligament and meniscus strains, bursitis, and chondromalacia. In the lower leg, 13 different diagnoses were offered with shinsplints and stress fractures heavily noted. Other injuries to the lower leg included muscle pulls, strains, and bruises. In the ankle, achilles tendinitis was the most frequent injury listed. The foot was also a problem site for injuries among Ironman competitors. Fourteen different diagnoses were offered for foot problems but with no real consistent problem area. Plantar fasciitis and blisters were listed but not to a great degree.

Based on the survey data in general, the knee is the most problematic anatomical injury site for triathletes. This observation comes as no surprise, for the two most demanding events in the triathlon offer trauma to the knee. A more controversial issue would be the differences and similarities of knee strain that the two sports impose on the knee. Edwards, as quoted earlier in this chapter, suggests that the triathlete's knee is pulled apart in the cycling movement and slammed together in running. But if you carefully examine the direction of force applied on the bicycle crank arms in Figure 6.8, you would find it difficult to confirm any pulling apart of the knee. A more likely rationale to the triathlete's knee syndrome would be the knee trauma offered over such a large range of motion. Greatest impact to the knee in running is when the leg is almost fully extended, but the cycling movement applies the greatest knee torque between 85 and 115 degrees. This will obviously place stresses over more of the articular surfaces of the patella, tibia, and femur.

Dave Scott (1983) suggests the order of training in the three sports may offer some relief from the trauma to the skeletal and muscular systems. Scott feels that most training should be done in a run-cycle-swim sequence. Scott also suggests allowing some recuperation time between events when in training.

Injury Prevention

There is nothing like an injury to defeat an athlete's goals, challenges, and outlook on life. Some of the most miserable people you want to be around are athletes in a cast. This is not hard to understand when you realize that so much of one's identity is wrapped up in pursuing goals of such an intense physical nature. To the athlete, the dream is inevitably one of winning, improving, or at least finishing. Injuries cut deep into fulfilling these dreams.

The athlete often gets so caught up in pursuing his/her dreams that injury prevention is overlooked. Like an automobile, most of us tend to the broken parts rather than follow any consistent plan of preventive maintenance. The old adage "the squeaky wheel gets the grease" is certainly true of how we care for our bodies as well.

The irony of the athletic injury problem is that we can do so much to prevent injuries from occurring in the first place. Some people never get injured. Certainly genetic makeup has some control over injuries and injury prevention, but more importantly, you, the athlete, create your own injury destiny. Therefore, the final section in this book is an attempt to develop a plan which can move you through your season of training and competition—injury-free.

To address this section, picture injury prevention on five levels. Each level builds on the next, so make sure the guidelines at each level are resolved before moving on to the next. The levels are as follows:

Level 1: Equipment

Level 2: Proper biomechanics

Level 3: Proper training

Level 4: Self-treatment of athletic injuries

Level 5: Professional treatment of athletic injuries

Level 1: Equipment

Before you first step down on the pedals or put one foot in front of the other, you need to make sure your equipment is in good repair and is properly adjusted. Wearing worn-out shoes, shoes that are not fitted properly, or using shoes not designed for your particular needs will almost certainly promote injuries.

Another equipment concern is to use a bicycle that is set up for your individual anatomy. Using a bike that is too big or too small will force your body into an abnormal position. Using a bike that is not adjusted properly will do the same. Those using cleated cycling shoes will need to make sure the cleat is precisely adjusted, as knee problems are often caused by cleats with the most-minute maladjustments. Please review the appropriate sections in chapters 6 and 7 for detailed writing on running and cycling shoes, as well as the sections on bicycle selection and adjustments.

Level 2: Proper Biomechanics

Once you are properly outfitted, your next concern is to refine the movements you intend to use in training. Chapters 5, 6, and 7 devote much attention to executing the proper swim, bike, and run movements. Training and competing with an unorthodox form create another setting for injuries. Proper movement mechanics are intentionally listed early on, so you won't practice and perfect an improper style of locomotion.

Level 3: Proper Training

Chapter 4 emphasized the need to progress gradually, to get proper rest, and to be alerted to the signs of overtraining. These are all very important concerns that have a tremendous bearing on injury prevention. Progression, for instance, can be a deceiving problem because the cardiovascular system often adapts at a faster rate than bones, joints, tendons, and ligaments. Although your mind and physical signs may be allowing you to move ahead, your joints are not and have no way of telling you this until it's too late. Make sure your progression is gradual and calculated. Dominguez (1983) suggests that distances never be increased more than 50% of what the body has adapted to. Progressions in 10% intervals are even more prudent.

Another suggestion would be to stagger-start your training program. Beginning your run and bicycle training at the same time causes tremendous trauma to the lower legs. Allowing the skeletal and muscular systems to adapt to one event before introducing the next would certainly decrease your chances of injury.

Finally, the prudent athlete will learn to listen to his/her body. So many serious injuries occur because one failed to yield to the body's warning signs. What are these warning signs? Pain, soreness, and swelling are the most obvious. Swelling is generally easy to discern. The swollen site is usually reddened, puffy, and warmer than the rest of the body. Swelling is a sure sign of injury and should not be neglected.

Soreness and pain may appear to be synonymous terms, but there is a distinction. Soreness is a natural response by the body whenever it is exposed to a new or higher-than-normal degree of physical exertion. We all experience soreness at the onset of our training programs. For the triathlete, soreness is at least a threefold experience in response to triple training. This soreness is called delayed soreness which is usually felt 24 to 48 hours after exercise. The cause of delayed soreness is only speculative; the most plausible explanation is injury to the tendons and muscle sheaths that wrap each muscle completely and also wrap smaller bundles within the muscle proper. Acute soreness is another type of soreness felt during exercise. Athletes identify this as a "burning" sensation, which in reality, is an inadequate supply of blood to the exercising muscle. Lactic acid is produced in these circumstances. Both types of soreness are a natural outcome of exercise and should not be viewed as a problem leading to injury.

Pain, on the other hand, is an actual response by the body to signal injury or potential injury. Built within the joints and muscles of the body are pain receptors which sense tissue damage occurring throughout the body. Pain serves as a warning sign and should be viewed as a protective mechanism. Realize that pain is a very relative issue, and the athlete's personality, for instance, will affect his/her perception of pain, particularly the degree to which one will accept or deny its presence.

Henderson (1977) classifies pain into various degrees which may guide the athlete through treatment.

> First degree pain—pain remains constant or increases as exercise continues, but without requiring the athlete to alter the form of the movement. Treatment at this level should be to eliminate the exercises which cause pain to increase. These are usually races, hard speedwork and the longest training bouts.
>
> Second degree pain—mild pain on easy workouts, severe pain with a disturbance of form on hard ones. Treatment would be to start each workout very slowly and cautiously. When pain builds to form-disturbing level, return to a rate in which form is not compromised.
>
> Third degree pain—impossible to exercise without great pain and a pronounced alteration of form in order to continue exercising. Treatment is to stop the exercises that cause this level of pain. As time passes, occasionally try the movement causing the pain to see if the pain reduces into a second or first degree level.

Trying to train through the pain is a crazy idea. Train through annoying sensations, but don't train through pain. Pain is destruction. The coined phrase "no pain—no gain" should be cashed in for a more prudent approach.

Level 4: Self-treatment of Athletic Injuries

Some injuries can be self-diagnosed and treated without the need and expense of professional intervention. The injuries in this classification include blisters, sprains, strains, and tendinitis that are at the first degree pain level. Treatment for minor sprains, strains, and tendinitis would be to reduce training intensity, duration, and frequency; then use ice on the injury site and aspirin to reduce swelling and pain. Blisters are caused by friction. Therefore, you need to identify and correct the cause of friction. Make sure you have shoes that fit well, wear socks that fit snugly and are clean and free of holes or ridges. Smear petroleum jelly over any developing "hot spots." Simple blisters can be punctured with a sterilized needle, carefully drained, and covered with sterile dressing. For a very comprehensive text on treatment of athletic injuries written for the lay reader, I recommend *Complete Book of Sports Medicine* by Dominguez (1979).

Level 5: Professional Treatment of Athletic Injuries

Seldom is the athlete willing to seek professional help without feeling some sense of failure or embarrassment. The natural response, therefore, is to avoid making the appointment in hopes the pain will go away. Rarely is this the case, and the athlete continues to make matters worse. Often what happens at the doctor's office is a diagnosis and a home treatment program is written. Seldom are you casted or directed to terminate all training. Professionals are becoming more aware that the athlete is not willing to go inactive, and alternative exercises are usually offered.

In general, any second or third degree pain should be professionally diagnosed. Better to deal with injury in a fetal state than to continue pushing until the injury is full grown. Knee pain, if not relieved from equipment and biomechanical changes and/or adjustments (Level 1 and 2), should be immediately referred to the professional.

Professional help can be sought from a number of people. The athletic trainer is always a great source with whom to begin. If the problem is too complex, this person will often refer you to a team physician or orthopedic surgeon. Most of these professionals are sensitive to an athlete's ever-pressing desire to continue training but experienced enough to tell the athlete what he/she needs to hear, not what he/she wants to hear.

Conclusions

The triathlon is new. It represents a fresh approach to three traditional sports. With any new endeavor comes much information on training concepts for competitors of all levels. You must critically evaluate these concepts according to your abilities, inabilities, and goals. Regardless of what you bring into the sport, please focus on your abilities and patiently work toward minimizing your inabilities. Remember that the primary goal of training should always be the same for everyone—to experience the joy and satisfaction of being physically fit and of finishing something which you start. With these goals in mind, everyone is a winner.

I hope this book serves as encouragement to all of you. Have fun pursuing triple fitness and do it with understanding and direction.

Bibliography

Alderman, B. (1974). *Psychological behavior in sport*. Philadelphia: W.B. Saunders Co.

Allen, B. (1979). Winged victory of Gossamer Albatross. *National Geographic*, **156**, 640-651.

American College of Sports Medicine. (1975). Position statement on prevention of heat injuries during distance running. *Medicine and Science in Sports*, **7**, vii.

Bates, S. & Town, G. (1985). *A survey of athletic injuries in triathletes*. Unpublished master's thesis, George Williams College, Downers Grove, IL.

Birch, D. & Veroff, J. (1966). *Motivation: A study of action*. Monterey, CA: Brooks/Cole.

Bohlmann, J. (1981). Injuries in competitive cycling. *The Physician and Sportsmedicine*, **9**(5), 117-124.

Brody, D. (1980). Running Injuries. *CIBA Clinical Symposia*, **32**(4).

Brunet, M., Haddad, R., & Porche, E. (1982). Rotator cuff impingement syndrome. *The Physician and Sportsmedicine*, **10**(12), 86-94.

Brynteson, P. & Sinning, W. (1973). The effects of training frequencies on retention of cardiovascular fitness. *Medicine and Science in Sports*, **5**, 29-33.

Burke, E. (1981). Ulnar neuropathy in bicyclists. *The Physician and Sportsmedicine*, **9**(4), 53-56.

Clement, D., Taunton, J., Smart, G., & McNicol, K. (1981). A survey of overuse running injuries. *The Physician and Sportsmedicine*, **9**(5), 47-58.

Costill, D.L. & Fink, W. (1974). Plasma volume changes following exercise and thermal dehydration. *Journal of Applied Physiology*, **37**, 679.

Costill, D.L., Fink, W., & Pollock, M. (1976). Muscle fiber composition and enzyme activities of elite distance runners. *Medicine and Science in Sports*, **8**(2), 96-100.

Costill, D.L. (1982). Fats and carbohydrates as determinants of athletic performance. In W. Haskell, J. Skala, & J. Whittam (Eds.), *Nutrition and athletic performance*. Palo Alto: Bull Publishing Co.

Costill, D.L., Thomason, H., & Roberts, E. (1973). Fractional utilization of the aerobic capacity during distance running. *Medicine and Science in Sports*, **5**(4), 248-252.

Costill, D.L., Gollnick, P.D., Jansson, E., Saltin, B., & Stein, B. (1973). Glycogen depletion pattern in human muscle fibers during distance running. *Acta Physiologica Scandinavica*, **89**, 374-383.

Costill, D.L., Sherman, W.M., Fink, W.J., Maresh, C., Witten, M., & Miller, J.M. (1981). The role of dietary carbohydrate in muscle glycogen resynthesis after strenuous running. *American Journal of Clinical Nutrition*, **34**, 1831-1836.

Councilman, J. (1977). *Competitive swimming manual.* Bloomington: Councilman Co. Inc.

Cundiff, D. (1979). Health fitness: Guide to a lifestyle. Dubuque: Kendall/Hunt Publishing Co.

Davis, M., Litman, T., Crenshaw, R., & Mueller, J. (1980). Bicycling injuries. *The Physician and Sportsmedicine,* **8**(5), 88-96.

De la Rosa, D. & Kolin, M. (1979). *The ten-speed bicycle.* Emmaus, Pa: Rodale Press.

Dominguez, R. (1979). *The complete book of sports medicine.* New York: Warner Books.

Dominguez, R. (1980). Shoulder pain in swimmers. *The Physician and Sportsmedicine* **8** (7), 36-42.

Doughty, T. (1983). *The complete book of long-distance and competitive cycling.* New York: Simon & Schuster.

Duffy, E. (1949). A systematic framework for the description of personality. *Abnormal Sociological Psychology,* **4,** 175-190.

Duffy, E. (1951). The concept of energy mobilization. *Psychological Review,* **58,** 30-40.

Duffy, E. (1962). *Activation and behavior.* New York: John Wiley & Sons.

Edwards, S. (1983). *The triathlon, a triple fitness sport.* Chicago: Contemporary Press.

FAO Nutritional Studies: (1970). *Amino acid content of foods and biological data on proteins.* No. **24,** Rome.

Faria, I., & Cavanagh, P. (1978). The physiology and biomechanics of cycling. *American College of Sports Medicine Series.* New York: John Wiley & Sons.

Firby, H. (1975). *Howard Firby on Swimming.* London: Pelham.

Gaston, E. (1979). Preventing biker's knees. *Bicycling,* July:50-53.

Gollnick, P., Armstrong, R., Sembrowich, W., Shepherd, R., & Saltin, B. (1972). Effect of training on enzyme activity and fiber composition of human skeletal muscle. *Journal of Applied Physiology,* **33**(3), 312-319.

Gollnick, P.D., Armstrong, R.B., Saltin, B., Saubert, C.W., Sembrowich, W.L., & Shepherd, R.E. (1973) Effect of training on enzyme activity and fiber composition of human skeletal muscle. *Journal of Applied Physiology,* **34,** 107-111.

Gross, A.C., Kyle, C.R. & Malewicki, D.J. (1983). The aerodynamics of human-powered land vehicles. *Scientific American,* **249**(6), 142-152.

Hamley E.J., & Thomas, V. (1967). Physiological and postural factors in the calibration of the bicycle ergometer. *Journal of Physiology,* **191,** 55-57.

Henderson, J. (1977). First aid for the injured. *Runner's World,* **12,** 32-37.

Hogan, C. (1983). How to start cross-training. *Bicycling,* **24**(9), 32-42.

Hogberg, P. (1952). How do stride length and stride frequency influence the energy output during running? *Int z Angew Physiol.,* **14,** 437.

Hoppeler, H., Luthi, P., Claassen, H., Weibel, E.R., & Howald, H. (1973). The ultrastructure of the normal human skeletal muscle: A morphometric analysis on untrained men, women and well-trained orienteers. *Pflugers Arch.,* **344,** 217-232.

Hultman, E., & Bergstrom, J. (1967). Muscle glycogen synthesis in relation to diet studied in normal subjects. *Acta Medisina Scandinavica,* **182,** 109-117.

Jenkins, D.J. et al. (1981). Glycemic index of foods: A physiological basis for carbohydrate exchange. *American Journal of Clinical Nutrition,* **34**(3), 362-366.

Kolin, M., & De la Rosa, D. (1979). *The custom bicycle.* Emmaus, Pa: Rodale Press.

Kranzley, G. (1983). Totally fit: The benefits of cross-training. *Bicycling,* **24**(9), 28-32.

Krissoff, W., & Ferris, W. (1979). Runners' injuries. *The Physician and Sportsmedicine,* **7,** 55-64.

Lemon, P. & Nagle, F. (1981). Effects of exercise on protein and amino acid metabolism. *Medicine and Science in Sports,* **13,** 141-149.

Levin, D. (1983, October). Gall, divided into three parts. *Sports Illustrated, Oct. 10, p.86.*

Magel, J., Foglia, G., McArdle, W., Gutin, B., Pechar, G., & Katch, F. (1974). Specificity of swim training on maximum oxygen uptake. *Journal of Applied Physiology,* **38,** 151-155.

Maglischo, E. (1982). *Swimming faster.* Palo Alto: Mayfield Publishing Co.

McArdle, W., Katch, F., and Katch, V. (1981). *Exercise physiology.* Philadelphia: Lea and Febiger.

McArdle, W., Magel, J., Delio, D., Toner, M., & Chase, J. (1978). Specificity of run-training on Vo_2max and heart rate changes during running and swimming. *Medicine and Science in Sports,* **10,** 16-20.

Miller, R., & Mason, J. (1964). Changes in 17-hydroxycorticosteroid excretion related to increased muscular work. *In Medical Aspects of Stress in the Military Climate.* Washington: Walter Reed Army Institute of Research, 137-151.

Morgan, W. (1979). Prediction of performance in athletics. In *Proceedings of Applied Sciences Symposium,* Klavora, P. (Ed.).

Morgan, W. (1980, July). The iceberg profile. *Psychology Today.* p. 93.

Morgan, W. & Johnson, R. (1978). Personality characteristics of successful and unsuccessful oarsmen. *International Journal of Sport Psychology,* 119-133.

Morgan, W. & Pollock, M. (1977). Psychologic characterization of the elite distance runner. In *Annals of the N.Y. Academy of Sciences,* **301,** 382-403.

Pechar, G., McArdle, W., Katch, F., Magel, J., & DeLuca, J. (1974). Specificity of cardiorespiratory adaptation to bicycle and treadmill training. *Journal of Applied Physiology,* **36,** 753-756.

Piehl, K. (1974). Time course for refilling of glycogen stores in human muscle fibers following exercise-induced glycogen depletion. *Acta Physiologica Scandinavica,* **90,** 297-302.

Powell, B. (1982). Correction and prevention of bicycle saddle problems. *The Physician and Sportsmedicine,***10**(10), 60-65.

Richardson, A.B., Jobe, F.W., & Collins, H.R. (1980). The shoulder in competitive swimming. *The American Journal of Sports Medicine* **8**(3), 159-163.

Roberts, J. & Alspaugh, J. (1972). Specificity of training effects resulting from programs of treadmill running and bicycle ergometer riding. *Medicine and Science in Sports,* **4,** 6-11.

Roy, S. & Irvin, R. (1983). *Sports medicine: Prevention, evaluation, management, and rehabilitation.* Englewood Cliffs: Prentice-Hall, Inc.

Saltin, B., & Karlsson, J. (1971). Muscle glycogen utilization during work of different intensities. *Advances in experimental medicine and biology,* **11,** 289-299.

Scott, D. (1983). Try it right. *Triathlon,* **1**(4), 27.

Scranton, P., & Stanitski, C. (1978). A simple look at major running overuse injuries. *Runner's World,* **13**(10), 108-111.

Selye, H. (1956). *The stress of life.* N.Y.: McGraw-Hill.

Shennum, P., & deVries, H. (1976). The effect of saddle height on oxygen consumption during bicycle ergometer work. *Medicine and Science in Sports,* **8**(2), 119-121.

Sherman, W. (1980). Dietary manipulation to induce muscle glycogen supercompensation: Effect on endurance performance. Unpublished master's thesis, Ball State University, Muncie, IN.

Sherman, W. (1983). Carbohydrates, muscle glycogen, and muscle glycogen supercompensation. In M. Williams (Ed.), *Ergogenic Aids in Sport,* pp. 3-13. Champaign, IL: Human Kinetics Pub. Inc.

Sherman, W.M., Costill, D.L., Fink, W.J., & Miller, J.M. (1981). The effect of exercise and diet manipulation on muscle glycogen and its subsequent utilization during performance. *International Journal of Sports Medicine,* **2,** 114-118.

Sinning, W., & Forsyth, H. (1970). Lower limb actions while running at different velocities. *Medicine and Science in Sports,* **2,** 28-34.

Sisson, M. & Hosler, R. (1983). *Triathlon training book.* Mountain View, CA: Anderson World Books.

Sloan, E. (1970). *The new complete book of bicycling.* N.Y: Simon and Schuster.

Smith, D.L., & Gaston, E.A. (1984). Coming back from injury: Debunking ''ankling.'' *Bicycling,* **25**(7), 39.

Stromme, S., Ingjer, F., & Meen, H. (1977). Assessment of maximal aerobic power in specifically trained athletes. *Journal of Applied Physiology: Respiratory Environmental Exercise Physiology,* **42,** 833-837.

Subotnick, S. (1977). A biomechanical approach to running injuries. *Annals New York Academy of Sciences.* **301,** 888-899.

Tipton, C.M., Matthes, R.D., Maynard, J.A., & Carey, R.A. (1975). The influence of physical activity on ligaments and tendons. *Medicine and Science in Sports,* **7,** 165-175.

Town, G., (1982). *Stride length and forward lean at various speeds in running.* Unpublished research, Wheaton College.

Town, G. & Sinning, W. (1982). Specificity of training effects as measured by serum enzymes. *Medicine and Science of Sports,* (abstract) **14**(2), 172.

VanHandel, P., Costill, D., & Getchell, L. (1976). Central circulatory adaptations to physical training. *Research Quarterly,* **47,** 815-823.

Whitt, F. & Wilson, D. (1983). Bicycling Science. Cambridge: MIT Press.

Woodard, J., & Town, G. (1983). The progressive metabolic and energy demands of triathlon competitors. *Medicine and Science in Sports and Exercise,* (Abstract) **15**(2), 126.

Index